M000283546

SOE Manual

SOE Manual

How to be an Agent in Occupied Europe

SPECIAL OPERATIONS EXECUTIVE

WILLIAM
COLLINS

The National Archives

William Collins
An imprint of HarperCollins*Publishers*
1 London Bridge Street
London SE1 9GF

WilliamCollinsBooks.com

HarperCollins*Publishers*
1st Floor, Watermarque Building, Ringsend Road
Dublin 4, Ireland

First published in Great Britain by William Collins in 2014

7

CONTENTS

SECURITY TALK.

(To be given by House Commandants to all students on arrival).

INTRODUCTION.

This is the most important part of your training. You will,
therefore, in your own interest be subject to strict security
rules.

GENERAL SECURITY PRECAUTIONS.

a. You will not be allowed to leave these grounds during the
course unless accompanied or specially instructed to do so.

(N.B:- i.   This does not apply to British Officers
undergoing non-operational training.

ii. House Commandants may use their discretion about recreational
walks; if in doubt they should refer to the Security Officer.)

b. You must never disclose at any time to anyone that you have
been at this School or at Beaulieu.

c. You must never recognise anyone whom you have met here if
you happen to meet them later on elsewhere, except on official
business.

LOCAL SECURITY RULES.

a. You will hand to me all identity documents now in your
possession for inspection. (Paybooks will be retained by me
during the course.)

b. You will hand to me any firearms, other weapons, cameras or
notebooks in your possession for retention during the course.

c. You will hand to me any money in excess of £5 and any

valuables for safekeeping until your departure. If you wish to
retain more than this sum you must obtain permission through
me from the Area Commandant. Failure to comply with this
rule will be regarded as contributory negligence in the event
of any loss. Any loss of kit or personal property must be
reported to me immediately.

d. Mail.

i. Outgoing. All letters will be handed to me in a stamped,
unsealed envelope for censoring. You must not make any
reference in your letters to the fact that they are censored.

You will use the Postal Box address already given to you or
the special arrangements for writing overseas.

Your letters will be posted in London.

ii. Incoming. All letters sent to you will be censored by the
Administrative Officer.

e. Telegrams. Telegrams, which may only be sent in cases of
urgency, will be handed to me for censorship and despatch.

f. Telephone. You will not use the telephone here or in the
locality. (This rule is only relaxed in special cases where H.Q.
desires to communicate urgently with a student.)

OPENING ADDRESS.

First of all let me bid you welcome. I hope that you will enjoy
your Course here and will find it helpful to you.

Now let's get to work. The purpose of the Organisation to
which you and I belong is Subversion. Subversion, properly
applied, is one of the most potent weapons one can use. It is

the fourth arm in modern warfare. What are its objects? They are
fourfold. I will give you these four headings, and I should like
you to pay particular attention to them as they are going to
govern most of what I am going to say to you this morning.

In the first place the objective is to damage the enemy's
material to the maximum extent, and also all his means of
communication and production. Modern warfare is almost entirely
dependent on material and communications. With every successive war
there is an increasing emphasis on machines and equipment, so much
so that no country without considerable industry at its call can
now dream of making war on a large scale. Therefore if you destroy
as many machines as possible, and damage the means of production,
you have gone a long way in hampering the enemy's effort.

The second objective is to strain the enemy's resources
of man-power. Towards the end of any long war the question
of man-power grows every day more vital. The Germans at this
moment are combing all their industries for men to put into
the field, and trying to replace them by foreign labour. Every
General seeks to employ the maximum amount of his resources at
the vital point of attack or danger. If a sufficient force can
be diverted to provide sentries, police, etc. the enemy's main
force is thereby weakened.

The third objective is to undermine the morale of the enemy.
In any long war the question of morale becomes an increasing
anxiety to leaders on both sides. If the morale of one side
cracks they lose the war, however many troops they may have left.
In the Autumn of 1918 the German troops were no longer fighting
in the same way as they had been previously. Why was that? Partly
because they were getting hungrier every day, partly because they
were getting tired of being kicked round by their N.C.O.'s - you
can stand that on a full stomach but it is not so easy on an

empty one - partly because they were getting misery letters from
their people at home. The morale of the German army was cracking
and, in consequence, the German army cracked. Anything we can
do to help along this process during the present war is going
to help to shorten it. There are plenty of methods. We must not
forget also the question of the Quislings, the collaborators. We
want them also to feel thoroughly uncomfortable.

Finally, there is the converse of this, to raise the morale of
the populations of the Occupied countries in order that they may
give us vital assistance when the right moment comes.

How do we achieve all this? There are plenty of methods to
produce all the effects we seek to bring about.

Damage to the enemy's material and means of production is, of
course, achieved by sabotage. Now there are various kinds, or
degrees, of sabotage and we can put these in an ascending scale.
There are at least four stages.

First of all there is the form of sabotage known as Passive
Resistance - an innumerable series of small acts which entail
virtually no risk to the perpetrators. The main principle is
non-co-operation - making the enemy feel that, while you are
keeping within the letter of his law, you are not in the least
won over by him and are only waiting your chance to liberate
yourselves. The enemy's life in Occupied countries should be made
as thoroughly uncomfortable as possible. He should be made to
feel an alien in a hostile environment. The Boche is an emotional
creature who cannot stand too much dislike.

All sorts of extra work can be created for him by over-caution
and especially by excessive zeal. The sort of zeal that sends him
anonymous denunciations of his collaborators, that sends him in

4

reports of non-existent unexploded bombs, elusive parachutists, etc. etc. If the thing is properly worked he need never suspect that he is being made a fool of.

The second stage we may call "industrial sabotage". Here there is some risk to the perpetrators, but it is not excessive. In the first place anything which can be done to prevent workers going to German factories is all to the good. As we have said, the Boche is anxious to recruit all the foreign labour he can in order to release his own men for the Army. Let us try to stop that. But one may as well take advantage of the fact that the workers will undoubtedly continue to flock to Germany, whether as volunteers or as conscripts, by including amongst them agents recruited specially for the purpose of starting sabotage in German factories. Here the possibilities are immense. The Germans claim to have already millions of foreign workers in Germany and only a very small percentage of these workers can really wish Germany to win the war.

In the third place, a great deal of damage can be done to factories and workshops by omitting to carry out certain essential functions, such as lubricating, or by substituting some abrasive for the real lubricant.

Lastly, workers can also hold up German production by a measurable percentage by causing waste and delay, and by excess of zeal or by over-caution. One can insist on a pedantic adherence to regulations or ask for frequent renewals and overhauls of machinery "so as to produce the best results". Too much time can be spent on doing any one job. One can always appear to insist upon an unnecessarily high standard. If every worker in every German factory were to leave his bench for the purposes of nature for double the usual period the effect on production would be quite measurable. One can also waste precious lubricants by over-lubrication, and time by too much attention to the safety regulations.

The third stage in sabotage might be called "minor sabotage", that is, isolated acts of definite destruction, such as blowing up a bridge, an electric transformer, wrecking power lines, etc. These do, of course, entail very considerable risk to the perpetrators but they have definite nuisance value.

Lastly we come to sabotage on the grand scale – "major sabotage" let us call it. This might involve the destruction of whole lengths of railway, bridges and roads in any given area. Naturally, there can be no attempt at concealment of these once they had occurred, although they would, naturally, be prepared under extremely secret conditions. They can only be accomplished by organised saboteur squads and they would be timed to coincide with same big event, such as invasion. So much for sabotage.

Now is that all that sabotage can accomplish? No. Successful sabotage also has the effect of straining the enemy's resources of man-power. This is effected in at least two different ways. All this faulty workmanship in factories which we have detailed needs putting right. It is not merely a question of duplicating labour – it may be far worse than that – a definite damage to the machine may have occurred by this careless lack of lubrication, for instance. Every attack which is made on rolling stock, and especially locomotives, must be the very devil for the enemy's repair shops which are already congested. In this way the enemy's resources of civilian man-power are being wasted.

But there is another aspect as well. Whenever a major act of sabotage occurs, the Gestapo swarm all over the district to make enquiries, and they nearly always result in recommendations for increased guards on these or other points. The more extra sentries we can get posted at points we do not intend to attack the better. If we can get whole police battalions diverted to certain areas it is better still.

How do we set about undermining the morale of enemy troops?
Well, there are several methods of political subversion about
which you will get details during the next few weeks. It is
no good trying to plant downright falsehoods on enemy troops,
you have no right to expect them to swallow them, but you can
work on grievances which they already have. You can fan their
dissatisfaction with their conditions, and also the anxiety they
must feel for their relations in North German towns which have
been heavily blitzed by the R.A.F. You can play on the feeling
of loneliness some of their troops must experience in remote
stations, and on the terror they must feel at the chance of being
stabbed in the back by the foreign population they are holding in
check when "the day" arrives. And you can make them almost sob at
the thought of all they are being deprived of.

Lastly, you can raise the morale of the population of the
occupied countries by various forms of propaganda which are
being used at this moment in every German-Occupied country every
day of the year. The object of this propaganda is to unify the
population in a common hatred of the Boche. Arising out of this
there should come the sort of non-co-operation with him which
is so important to us. One can implant in them a conviction
amounting to certainty that the Allies will win - from that
should spring an active desire to help that victory forward.

These, then, are the objects which we seek to attain by
subversion, and I have just detailed some of the methods by
which they can be achieved. It is obvious, however, that all
these effects will be haphazard, and therefore largely wasted,
if they are not all bound up in a general plan, which covers
all activities and times them all to fit in, like a railway
schedule. Each single act of sabotage, of propaganda, or of
political subversion ought to be part of a definite plan of
attack.

The plan naturally varies with each country and there are several factors which govern it. There is first of all, naturally, military strategy, for all our subversive efforts are governed by what the main plan of attack may be - and subversion is only one part of a very large whole. It is no use, for instance, laying on an ambitious plan of sabotage for a country which the High Command has decided at the last moment not to attack - unless it is a deliberate plan of diversion.

It is naturally also influenced by the German economic situation. For instance, one of the main German weaknesses at the moment is communications, and that is why they are so constantly attacked both by the R.A.F. and saboteurs. Then there is the question of the political situation. The relations between the Allies and some so-called neutral countries are so delicate that no subversive operations can be contemplated in those countries for the time being, even though it is apparent that they may be the next on the list for attack by the Germans. There is also the nature of the country to be considered - the density of its population, and the degree of industrialisation. It is obvious that the plan for small densely populated and highly industrialised countries, such as Belgium and Holland, would be different from that for the deserts of Libya - if there is one.

Lastly the attitude of the civil population may make a considerable difference to the plan. In some countries secret organisations already exist in fairly large numbers and they may have to be taken into consideration. The attitude of some Occupied countries is far more virile than that of others, who are inclined to lie down and do nothing about it. In some parts of the country there may even be an active pro-Nazi element. All these factors have to be weighed.

The general policy in whatever country you may be sent to

an be divided into two phases - the pre-invasion phase and the nvasion phase. Let us take the pre-invasion phase first.

The first essential is to organise each country, area by rea. Naturally the organisation in each country will vary normously according to factors of geography, population and ndustry, so that no two countries will be entirely alike. 'or the same reasons the organisation inside each area may be xtremely simple, or, on the other hand, it may be a fairly omplex organisation, closely knit together. In addition to he factors I have already mentioned, there is the dominating actor of the German counter espionage control. It is their ctivities which mostly dictate what kind of organisation ne can stage. Then there is the question of the native rganisations already working inside the country - the so-alled secret armies. Here again the policy varies so much rom country to country and according to the run of the war, hat it is impossible to lay down any universal principle. In ome countries organisers may be asked to go out as pioneers nd organise some guerrilla bands, with various objectives to e attacked when the "day" comes. In other countries agents re sent out regularly to form part of the powerful secret rganisations already existing, and to fill niches in those rganisations, such as arms instructors, sub-area organisers, /T operators, etc. Yet in other countries, the organisation of hich you form a part functions entirely separately from these rganisations, which are probably too well known to the Boche. ut even in these cases some attempt must be made to take note f these local societies and to assess their value.

Naturally most of your activities will form a preparation for he great day when your countries come to be liberated, and the nvasion phase should, therefore, see your activities at maximum tretch. Everything depends on the secrecy and efficiency with

9

which these preparations are made. The more that each separate operation can be prepared, and even possibly rehearsed, the better it is likely to go off when the day comes.

Here again the operational orders naturally vary considerably for each country, so that it is impossible to lay down any universal plan to apply to all countries. Nevertheless the activities, some part of which you will probably be asked to prepare for, will include such things as:-

a).   A whole series of combined attacks on the enemy's rail, road and telecommunications. If, for instance, it were possible to isolate completely, for even 48 hours, a vital strategic centre 50 miles behind the enemy's lines just at the moment when the Allies were landing, just think what a gift this would be to the Allied commander. If it were impossible for the enemy to get his troops up to the threatened spot at the right moment because his communications were temporarily sabotaged, it might make all the difference to the success or failure of the operations - in that sector at all events.

b).   Demolishing important river bridges which are vital to the enemy's communications. Or, conversely, preventing the enemy from doing so when he wishes to prevent the Allies from advancing. The campaign of 1940 in the Low Countries showed what tragic results to the defence can result from a single important bridge failing to be demolished. And it is about time that the Germans had some of their own medicine.

c).   Attacks on enemy H.Q.'s, telephone installations, wireless vans, etc. A small gang of disciplined men can very soon deal with even an important enemy H.Q. if the operation is thoroughly studied and planned beforehand. If the sentries are attacked at exactly the right moment and the men in the

10

uard-room overwhelmed, one can very soon over-run a whole H.Q.
uilding by running down the corridors and throwing bombs or
renades in each room. They are fairly effective weapons in
hose conditions.

d). Blocking roads which must be used by the enemy's
ransport, but care must be taken not to block roads which may
e required by the advancing Allies. It has been rightly pointed
ut that it is impossible to block any road for more than a
ertain time. Nevertheless if the enemy had to vacate a town at
 moment's notice, with a large amount of transport, and then
ave to deal with road blocks, or possibly road craters, it
ight make all the difference to them, more especially if the
ky was then filled with bombing aeroplanes which left them no
espite.

e). The question of the civil population is a very
mportant one, for it was their action in pouring out on to all
he roads before the advancing Germans in 1940 that seriously
andicapped the Allies in their attempts to deal with the
erman invasion. Here again detailed plans will be worked out
n due course to tell the civil population what they can do to
elp, and especially what they can avoid doing to hinder. No
oubt the B.B.C. will play a large part in this, but one cannot
ely on the civilian population having receivers in an area
hreatened by invasion, and it may well be that your services
ay prove extremely useful in coping with an urgent problem of
his kind.

Where does the organiser fit into all these schemes? The
rganiser is the key man in all of them, and it is on his work
nd organisation that the smooth carrying out of all the plans
epends. You will have seen enough from what I have told you
o realise that any one organiser has only a very small part -

11

although an important one - in a vast organisation, and that any work he carries out is only a minute part of a big general plan. You will therefore appreciate the absolute necessity of team work. Too much individualism on the part of any one organiser might go far to wreck the plan.

The roles of the organiser are various. More often than not he is sent into the field with a specific mission to carry out. He may be given a target to demolish; he may be asked to foment industrial unrest in a particular area; he may be asked to organise a small guerrilla band in a certain district. On the other hand, he may be sent out as a pioneer with instructions to organise a certain area. In that case, he starts from scratch. He will have to make a survey of his area, and decide what are the most suitable targets to attack, and what type of organisation is best adapted to the purpose. If he is working not too far from this country, and is in fairly close touch, he will probably report back either by W/T or by letter, or, more likely still, return on a short visit. On the other hand, if the spot to which he goes is at the other end of the earth, we may not see him back again before the end of the war, and he will have to use his own initiative throughout.

It is obvious he can do none of these things unless he is properly trained and equipped for his task. That is why you have come to Beaulieu. During the next . . . . weeks you will have the task of studying the underground life in every aspect - starting with the moment at which you arrive on the ground and disengage yourself from your parachute. You will have to learn how to bury it safely, and to start your new life in your new surroundings. We shall be discussing with you every kind of measures for your own safety - the importance of having the right story to tell, the right kind of job to do, and how to lead your life most in accordance with those facts. We shall teach you how to build up

12

our organisation from zero. There is only one word of warning I
wish to make here. If you follow conscientiously in the field all
that we teach you here, we cannot guarantee your safety, but we
think that your chance of being picked up is very small. Remember
that the best agents are never caught. But some agents when they
get out into the field find it apparently much easier than they
expected, and they are inclined to relax their precautions. That
is the moment to beware of. Never relax your precautions, and
never fool yourself by thinking that the enemy are asleep. They
may be watching you all the time, so watch your step.

INDIVIDUAL SECURITY.

. INTRODUCTION.

a) Security must be the first consideration of the agent.
Unless he has taken the necessary precautions for his own
safety it is useless for him to attempt any subversive work
alone or in conjunction with other people.

b) Apart from the danger to the individual agent his arrest
may jeopardise the safety of an organisation with which he is
in contact.

c) The agent, unlike the soldier, who has many friends,
is surrounded by enemies, seen and unseen. He cannot even
be certain of the people of his own nationality who are
apparently friendly. The agent must, therefore, remember that,
like primitive men in the jungle, he has only his alertness,
initiative and observation to help him. He has to look after
himself but we can prepare him for this by training.

d) Despite the apparent difficulties the agent can train
himself to be security-minded and by self-discipline make the
taking of precautions an automatic process (cf. crossing the

road). He should, at the same time, beware of the danger of over-confidence when he sees little evidence of measures being taken against him.

2. RULES.

The following rules should be studied and followed by the agent and passed on to any one he recruits:

a) Cover.

b) Information.

c) Alertness.

d) Inconspicuousness.

e) Discretion.

f) Discipline.

g) Planning for emergency.

a) Cover. It is essential to have a comprehensive cover story for his past and every action, and to do nothing which might jeopardise it. This is dealt with in detail in another lecture.

b) Information. This is the basis of all the agent's work. As much as possible is provided before departure but the agent must check and supplement it on arrival. For the purposes of self-protection, information will be required on:

i. Conditions and regulations in the agent's area.

ii. Enemy methods and personnel.

e) Alertness.

i. The agent cannot rely on the law for protection; on the

contrary, he is opposed to it, and must depend on alertness and observation, e.g. must see danger early (old friend in the street, or policeman checking papers) so that he may have time to avoid it.

ii. He should not only observe things but also make deductions from them, e.g. papers moved suggesting someone has been in his room; a smell of real coffee suggesting someone connected with black market; familiar voice or face suggesting that the agent is being followed.

iii. Combined with alertness of mind, the agent should develop a good memory; the ability to remember a face, details of instructions, plans laid some time previously, is an essential requisite for the agent, who should commit as little as possible to writing.

d) Inconspicuousness.

The agent should avoid attracting attention to himself by:

i. Observing all rules and regulations. Small infringements may bring the agent into contact with the police and may lead to further investigations. Little danger in this for the person not engaged in clandestine activity, but for the agent it is unnecessary contact with the police. He should, therefore, be a "model citizen".

ii. Personal behaviour. Under this heading consider physical appearance (hands, hair, etc.), clothes, friends (avoid persons suspected by the police, Jews, Communists, etc.), tastes, amusements, etc. The agent should merge into the background and act in the same way as those around him. This does not mean perpetual silence – which might be even more conspicuous – but natural behaviour. Build up good reputation – be pleasant to people and avoid annoying them. Conform to local conditions.

e) Discretion.

The agent must not give himself away by carelessness.

i. In conversation. The agent should not:

confide in friends just to relieve the strain on nerves;

answer questions in such a way as to arouse curiosity;

tell people more than they need know, no matter how important or how close the association;

adopt a "hush-hush" attitude (vanity is usually the cause of this), or an atmosphere of importance;

mention facts which he is not supposed to know;

mention isolated facts at different times which can be pieced together;

be led into making compromising statements, e.g. by pro-German remark.

ii. With incriminating material or documents. The agent must not leave about, and, as far as possible, must not carry, incriminating documents, e.g. names, addresses, notes. Remember that even a tram ticket may in some circumstances be an incriminating document. A daily check of the contents of one's pockets is essential and all unnecessary documents must be destroyed at once.

iii. Behaviour. The agent must observe self-discipline, e.g. be able to control his reactions in routine controls or if accidents occur. Practise moderation in drink, care in relations with women, avoid celebration after success, etc.

f) Discipline.

It is essential to security as well as to efficiency that

an agent should obey his chief's orders exactly and without dispute.

g) Planning for Emergency.

The agent must foresee emergency and plan in advance the action to be taken.

i. Arrange alternatives in case of accident or misunderstanding, e.g. alternative R.V. if the first is not kept.

ii. Prepare for any sudden difficulty, e.g. prearranged conversation in talking to colleague in case of interruption.

iii. Prepare signs by which he can warn colleagues of the fact that he is in danger.

iv. Plans must be laid for eventual flight if he comes under grave suspicion, and a suitable hide-out prepared. Any necessary false papers and clothes for this disappearance should be readily available, including a reserve supply of money. Cover story advisable to explain the disappearance. Simple disguise.

3. CONCLUSION.

The security precautions outlined above should be put into practice as soon as the agent enters the organisation and starts his training. Although the danger of German espionage in this country is not so great, all precautions should be taken. It is also necessary to know how to deal with friends and other persons who might be curious.

By starting at such an early stage the agent is also getting into the habit of thinking along security lines and preparing himself for his work in the field. He must remember that secrecy, even with those nearest to him, and in whom he has the most confidence, is essential for his safety.

C O V E R.

1. DEFINITION.

Your cover is the life which you outwardly lead in order to
conceal the real purpose of your presence and the explanation
which you give of your past and present. It is best considered
under the heads; Past, Link between Past and Present, Present
and "Alibis".

2. YOUR PAST.

Before your departure, with the assistance of your Section
Officers, you will probably prepare a story of your past life
up to the time of your arrival. But you cannot always arrange
a complete story before leaving; furthermore you may have to
change part, or all, of your cover story when you are actually
in the field and know what your circumstances are to be.
Nevertheless you must be able to give some account of yourself
if questioned immediately after your arrival.

In inventing or amending your cover story, or that of another
agent, the following points should be considered:-

a. Identity.

i. Your Own.

Advantages: Your story will be mainly true.

Only a limited period will have to be explained away.

Records will confirm your statements.

Disadvantages: The subversive part of your history may be

18

known to the enemy or to persons who may give you away. This is usually the case with escapees.

ii.   That of a Real Person, Distant or Dead.

Advantages: The story, being real, will be self-consistent. Records will confirm at least part of it.

Disadvantages: People acquainted with the person whom you are impersonating may give you away. You may have incomplete information about this person's past life, so that your statements may be shown to be untrue. The person may be suspected without your knowing it.

iii. Wholly Fictitious.

Advantages: Less chance of entanglements and wider scope.

Disadvantages: Records will not confirm your story.

In some cases agents have to assume different identities in different places. This should be avoided as far as possible, because it leads to contradictions. N.B. The danger of two identity cards.

b.   History.

i.   Whatever your identity, your story must be plausible and not indicate any connexion with subversive activity.

ii.   It should be based, as far as possible, on the facts of your own life or that of the person whom you are impersonating. Do not introduce places or events which you do not know nor refer to knowledge which you have not. (Do not claim to know of engineering if you do not.)

iii. Pay particular attention to that part of your story which is linked with the details shown in your documents. They may be examined closely.

iv.   Your recent history is of most interest to the police.
It is also most difficult to invent satisfactorily. Particular
care should be devoted to its preparation.

v.   Although a complete mastery of details is essential in
the preparation of the story, vagueness is often desirable
when repeating it, especially in the case of more distant and
less important parts.

c.   Documents.

These are supplied by your Section and will be as
nearly perfect as possible. The following points must be
remembered:-

i.   You must know how you would have obtained them if they
had been issued to you legally.

ii.   All the documents you need cannot always be produced
in this country, e.g. those which change frequently, such as
ration cards in some countries.

iii. The falsity of forged documents is always ultimately
detectable if counterfoils exist, especially if they are numbered
consecutively. It may take a long time to establish this falsity.

iv.   Perfect documents can only be obtained through official
sources in the field.

d.   Clothes and Effects.

i.   Do not take anything with you which does not fit your
story.

ii.   Your effects can sometimes furnish valuable corroborative
evidence of the "truth" of your background cover. e.g.
unofficial papers, tickets, bills, local products, etc.

e.   Change of Appearance.

i.   To support assumed character (rough hands for workman.)

ii.   To avoid recognition if you are going among people who know you.

N.B. Application of disguise is dealt with in a special lecture.

f.   Final Search.

You must search your person and residence for traces which link you with your "other self":-

i.   Before your departure.

ii.   Whenever you change your cover story.

iii. If you wish to conceal some recent activity.

iv.   If you are about to undertake some special subversive act.

3. FROM PAST TO PRESENT.

As soon as you arrive you must adopt a cover life to account for your presence. Your cover story for your past must merge naturally into this.

a.   From the beginning start completing the details of the cover story of your past. Really do the things you say you have done. Really go to the places you say you have been to. This will serve a double purpose:-

i.   You will obtain the information which you would have had, had your story been true, e.g. see the towns, learn their recent history, etc. With this knowledge you can support and, if necessary, modify your background cover.

ii.   You can manufacture evidence confirming your background cover, e.g. make acquaintance in the places you go to, possess things coming from these places, etc.

b.   Build up also your present cover background by innocent
and inconspicuous actions to which reference can be made
later. It may be useful to make innocent acquaintances, etc.

4. YOUR PRESENT.

This is the life which you lead and the story which you will
tell about that life to account for your presence. It may be
planned with the help of your Section Officers before your
departure. Or you may have to work it out for the first time
after your arrival. In any case, your ostensible present must
be consistent with your alleged past.

a.   Maintenance of Cover.

i.   Name. Always sign correctly and respond to it
immediately.

ii.   Consistency in General. Your personality and general
conduct must fit your cover background, e.g.:-

Expenditure must accord with ostensible income.

Volume and nature of correspondence must fit your social
circumstances.

Character of friends and acquaintances must accord with your
cover personality.

Documents, clothing, possessions; etc. must be suitable.

Manners, tastes, bearing, accent, education and knowledge must
accord with your ostensible personality.

iii.   Concealment of Absence from your Country.

Avoid foreign words, tunes, manners, etc. Avoid slang which
has developed among your countrymen in Britain.

Avoid showing knowledge or expressing views acquired in Britain.

Conform with all new conditions which have arisen, observe new customs and acquire the language which has developed in your country.

a.   Cover Occupation.

It is advisable for you to have, or pretend to have, a cover occupation. (A real one is best, but sometimes their subversive activity does not permit agents to do other work.) An occupation is necessary:-

i.   To account for presence in locality.

ii.   To explain the source of livelihood.

iii. To avoid, if possible, conscription for work in Germany or elsewhere.

In selecting a cover occupation, bear in mind the possibilities of having:-

An unregistered job, such as student, stamp dealer, or,

An imaginary job. In this case it is an advantage if you have a real employer to vouch for you.

Your range of choice of occupation is restricted by certain factors. Some of these factors apply also to an imaginary job. Consider the following:-

Some jobs involve special investigation of credentials and/or restriction of liberty.

The job which you select should afford you cover and facilities for your activity. Consider hours, pay, movement, technical facilities, e.g. transport, storage, access, etc.

You must have adequate technical qualifications.

c.   Conclusion.

Good background cover is hard to build up and easily
destroyed. It is essential to your relations with the general
public. Never sacrifice such cover once acquired if you can
possibly avoid it.

Remember, however, that a serious investigation is likely to
break down your background cover by exposing the falseness
of your documents or statements about your past life. Always,
therefore, avoid trouble with the authorities. Have a ready
story to account for everything.

In some cases an ostensible lawful existence is impossible.
Then you must live underground. Be inconspicuous. Avoid
officials. Vary your appearance, habits, haunts, routes, etc.
Produce one story or another as the occasion demands.

5. "ALIBI".

a.   Nature of "Alibi".

In addition to your cover background, you must have an
explanation ready for every subversive act, however small,
e.g. conversation, journey. Such alibis are more important
than your background cover. If they are good no further
enquiries will be made.

You may be questioned about your activity in many different
circumstances and have to conceal its true nature, e.g. when
obtaining permits, telephoning by regular or snap controls,
through infringing regulations or being called as a witness,
through suspicious activity when under surveillance.

b.   Construction of an "Alibi".

Remember the following points:-

i.   Plausibility. If you give a plausible explanation of your conduct no further investigation is likely. An unplausible one will be investigated and must, therefore, be watertight. A plausible story justifies a friendly policeman in letting you go. If your story is not plausible he may not dare to do so in case you are an agent provocateur.

ii. Detail. Decide on the "facts" which must be prepared in detail and those which can be left vague, e.g. people remember times of rendezvous trains, etc., but not when they have finished meals. If you can remember a time exactly there is usually a reason for it, e.g. because you checked your watch with the town hall clock or you turned on the wireless for a particular programme, and it is occasionally a good thing to mention this casually.

iii. Self-Consistency. Your "alibi" must be consistent with your circumstances, especially those immediately ascertainable, e.g. clothes, general appearance, special knowledge, activity.

iv. Cover Background. For choice your "alibi" should be consistent with your main cover background, but you may have to manufacture special background for the occasion.

v.   Truth. The "alibi" should be as near the truth as possible, provided that it is not suspicious. Time can be expanded. Dates of events can be transposed. If you do this make sure you allow for different circumstances on different days, e.g. do not say you had been to the market if there is no market on the day for which you give your alibi, although there was one on the day the events of which you have transposed. Furthermore have a story ready in case you are asked about your movements for the day the events of which you have moved. Where the story is quite untrue the false parts can often be rehearsed. Cf. Build up of cover (above). It is dangerous to tell a story entirely untrue.

vi.   Dead End. In so far as is possible the story
should be closed. It should leave few openings for further
investigation. Links with outside persons, events or places
are dangerous.

vii. Consistency with Others. If you are going to mention
people who will corroborate your story you must arrange this
very carefully. Attention should be paid to the following
points:-

1.   Your stories should support each other without being
exactly alike. In particular you should not all be vague on
the same points, and precise on the same points.

2.   Consider the possibility of arranging answers to
unforeseen questions in a particular way, e.g. who took
the initiative in a particular action. But if the period is
fairly long divide it up so that A took the initiative during
the first hour, B during the second etc. unless there is a
particular reason for one person taking the lead e.g. because
he was host, or because he knows the town better than the
others.

viii. Discreditable Story. Consider the possibility of using as
an "alibi" a discreditable story. Sometimes this can be used
as an alternative upon which to fall back should the first
story break down.

N.B. Provided that you have not been questioned about your
alibi, you can change it freely; e.g. one to explain what you
are going to do, a second to explain what you are doing and a
third to account for what you have done.

c.   False Confession.

Have ready, in case you are caught red-handed a story that you
are engaged in subversive activity, but which protects your

organisation, minimises your role and conceals the fact that you are a parachutist. If possible quote the names of friends who are dead or in safety, to support your story.

INTERROGATIONS.

1. GENERAL.

Interrogations can be divided into three classes:-

a)   Carried out by Local Police. Generally on account of infringement of minor regulations. Usually confined to four simple questions:-

i)   Who are you?

ii)   Where do you come from?

iii) What papers have you?

iv)   What are you doing?

If able to satisfy the police on these points, suspect is generally released. In the event of any discrepancies he will be subjected to further interrogation.

Immediately after arrival or after any parachute operation in the neighbourhood, you should be prepared to answer plausibly these questions:-

i)   Where are you?

ii)   Where do you come from?

iii) How did you come?

iv) Where are you going?

v) Who is and where is the last person you spoke to who knows you personally?

vi) Give details of this locality.

b) Carried out by Specialist Police. Indicate type of police. To find out whether a person is definitely suspect, e.g. through having failed to satisfy the local police in the preliminary interrogation. Suspect will have to satisfy the police that his "story" and papers are genuine. His replies will probably be checked. Attempts may be made to catch him out by producing facts which he thinks the Police do not know.

c) Carried out by Gestapo, or equivalent authority, after arrest. For a person seriously suspected, e.g. because he has failed to satisfy local police and Gestapo in previous interrogations or because he has been caught red-handed. This interrogation may last from 24 hours to many months. Methods are manifold but aim is single - to extract a confession. No rules; nothing barred; "all-in".

2. INTERROGATION METHODS.

a) Before Interrogation.

i) Sudden but polite arrest on pretext of unimportant enquiry, followed by indefinite detention to prevent warning of associates.

ii) Sudden arrest in the middle of the night when vitality is at its lowest.

iii) Complete house and body search. Exhaustive enquiries

about suspect's life and activities in order to collect as much evidence as possible before interrogation.

iv)   Treatment in prison all part of interrogation plan, e.g. bad food, alternatively good food, comfort and discomfort, comparative liberty and solitary confinement, promising visits from friends, etc. Object is to break down moral strength before actual questioning.

b)   During Interrogation.

Every effort will be made to make the prisoner feel ill at ease both physically and mentally. Some of the following methods may be tried:-

i)   Prisoner facing strong light; unable to see examiner properly.

ii)   Prisoner may be made to assume uncomfortable or humiliating postures.

iii) Prisoner seated on uncomfortable chair. Not allowed to eat, drink or smoke while examiners indulge in all three.

iv)   Prisoner may be wholly or partly stripped sometimes in the presence of members of the opposite sex.

v)   Prisoner may be at one end of a long bare room and this isolation may be emphasised by the interrogators pretending to ignore the prisoner.

vi)   Single interrogation may continue indefinitely so that prisoner becomes exhausted.

vii) Prisoner may be threatened with the firing squad in the hope he will defy his "executioners" and admit his guilt.

viii) Prisoner's family may be threatened.

ix) Prisoner will be insulted and menaced. Interrogators may try to discover prisoner's susceptibilities so as to direct their insults with telling effect.

x) Unsatisfactory prisoners may be beaten up.

3. TYPES OF INTERROGATORS.

Examination may be carried out by two or more persons acting simultaneously or, more usually, in sequence, e.g.:-

First Interrogator often the "bully" type who tries to make prisoner either angry or frightened; impresses on him the terrible power of the Gestapo (*wir wissen alles*); threatens, throws things about.

Second Interrogator puts clear, concise, sharp questions. If results are unsatisfactory, prisoner may be "beaten up".

Third Interrogator, friendly, offering food, drink, cigarettes and apologising for rough treatment; will try to lull prisoner into indiscretion. He may attempt to find out prisoner's hobbies and interests and either discuss them with him or send for another interrogator who knows a good deal about them. Probably most dangerous type.

N.B. There may also be present a compatriot of the prisoner. He may act as interpreter or may say nothing. His presence may alter the prisoner's attitude, e.g. by reason of local knowledge.

4. TECHNIQUE OF QUESTIONING.

i) Continually referring back to the same question with a different method of approach.

ii) Suggestion that prisoner has been let down by his friends or is shielding someone else.

iii) Another agent may be brought in and confronted with the prisoner.

iv)   Showing prisoner a "confession" signed by collaborator.

v)   Reconstruction of offence exaggerating prisoner's share in it.

vi)   Misquotation of previous replies. If prisoner accepts it directly or by implication he will be accused of lying and bullied until he is completely confused.

vii) Production of plans of places where incidents have taken place, or relation of incidents with slight errors. Then later prisoner is obliged to reproduce plan or relate story in the hope he will unconsciously correct errors or fill in details not mentioned.

viii) Giving prisoner papers to sign after exhausting day of examination.

ix)   Use of ether.

COUNTER-MEASURES.

a)   During the detention.

i)   If in same prison cell as other members of organisation, beware of microphone. Do not discuss your work unless you can do so by signs or under cover of some other noise.

ii)   If allowed to mix with other detained persons, say nothing; danger of "stool-pigeons". A favourite trick of stool-pigeons is to appear very miserable, you feel so sorry for them that in trying to cheer them up you say too much.

iii) Beware of friendly warders who offer to help you, unless you have proof they are working for your organisation.

iv)   If you are released be careful and do not contact your
organisation directly; release may be only temporary to watch
your movements.

v)   Always try to appear clean, neat and, if possible, well
dressed. Do a little P.T. regularly.

b)   During Questioning.

i)   Speak slowly, clearly and firmly. Do not answer simple
questions immediately and hesitate with the more difficult
ones. Similarly keep an even level of preciseness i.e. do
not overdo the detail in replies to easy questions and then
"forget" everything with difficult ones.

ii)   Remember that shouting, bullying, coaxing, joking,
sentimentality etc. is all an act to make you afraid, angry,
hilarious or sentimental and thereby lessen your vigilance.

iii)   Do not be clever or abusive. Create impression of being
an averagely stupid, honest citizen, trying his best to answer
questions intelligently. Interrogators are not impressed
by tears or heroics. In occasional cases a bold attitude
sometimes impresses interrogators; you must judge them as you
see them. But always be civil.

iv)   Avoid replies that lead to further questions. All
your answers should end in a cul-de-sac. Do not help the
interrogators by adding unsolicited information.

v)   Deny everything you cannot explain. Do not attempt
to get round difficulties by altering or embellishing your
stories.

vi)   Never confess because of the supposed confession of
a colleague. It is useful to arrange for a code sign or
signature (normal) on any statement extracted by force. Even
if a comrade recognises you deny that you know him, or if you

are supposed to know him deny all knowledge of his subversive work. Even if he has talked under pressure the Germans know that such confessions are often false.

vii) Do not express personal affection or interest in anybody.

viii) Pretend to be worn out before you are. Then they are likely either to leave you alone for a bit or to ask the really important questions, in which case they are inclined to believe your answers.

ix) If you speak German, provided such knowledge agrees with your cover, it is probably best to admit you understand a little or say you learnt it at school but have forgotten most of it. Otherwise they may catch you out with traps. But say you do not know enough to understand or answer questions because then,

either the Germans will have to interrogate in your language which puts them at a disadvantage or else they will have to use an interpreter which is less effective, and gives you more time to think as the questions are put twice;

they may talk to each other about you and you may get useful information;

if you contradict yourself you can blame the interpreter.

If you speak German really well, and this accords with your cover, in some cases it may pay to admit it. It tends to dispose them slightly in your favour.

x)   Demand to know with what you are charged and who is your accuser.

xi) Organisers should fix a time limit up to which prisoners should try to hold out, in order to allow that part of the

organisation with which the prisoner was in contact to put
emergency plans into operation.

xii) If you are forced to talk try to warn your comrades.

xiii) Do not be put off if they produce details you did
not think they knew - names, addresses, or even details of
training in Great Britain. It is usually bluff.

xiv) If you are forced to speak have ready a story minimising
your role, which you can support by mentioning the names of
colleagues who are dead or in safety or addresses which have
been abandoned.

xv)   Beware of apparently foolish interrogator of whom you
may think you have got the better. This may be a trap to tempt
you to boast of your cleverness in circumstances where your
boastings will be reported.

CONCLUSION.

Have a simple straightforward story and stick to it. And above
all go on denying at any price.

A. 8, 9 & 10
February 1944

KNOW YOUR ENEMY.

1. INTRODUCTION.

In order to live in your country you must know the forces and
methods by which the enemy makes resistance difficult, viz.

(a)   C.E. personnel used, uniformed and secret police, spies,
etc.

(b) Regulations imposed on the general public, which restrict the agent's activities or may cause him to become conspicuous.

(c) Detective measures, devised to enforce these regulations and to trap agents of resistance.

(d) Threats, promises, reprisals, and bribes, designed to persuade or frighten the population into preventing or denouncing subversive acts or refraining from them.

C.E. PERSONNEL USED. (to be mentioned briefly, with reference to C. Lectures).

German Police,

German Troops,

National Police,

National Sabotage – guards etc.

Fascist bodies specially formed,

Individual Nazis.

Criminals released for the purpose.

Blackmailed persons.

Agents arrested and released.

P.O.W. or workers returned from Germany.

Persons tempted by rewards.

REGULATIONS.

(a) Directed against subversive activity.

(b) Imposed for economic, moral, and other reasons (against black market; against girls going out alone).

(c) Previous laws and regulations of the country.

Infringement of any of those may make the agent conspicuous or suspect.

(Here briefly mention routine controls - snap and permanent and spies, to be dealt with more fully later.)

(Under each of the following headings quote the regulations of the student's country, with advice for that country.)

A. Identity.

Identity card compulsory in most occupied countries. Entered in archives. Particulars on it kept up to date. How obtained officially. Occasions on which it must be produced (travel, telegraphing, etc.). Special cards for Prohibited Areas.

Additional documents confirming identity often carried and sometimes obligatory (birth certificate, marriage certificate. military, marine, and demobilisation papers, etc.).

How to get false papers (through organisation, from patriotic official; by pretence of loss of identity card); how to do with unsatisfactory papers or none (approach police with question; scratched mica cover; photo of naked lady).

B. Residence.

Generally speaking residence is registered and change of residence must be notified to the authority.

(a) Possibilities.

i. Hotels. Regulations. Freedom of movement and inconspicuousness, but watching by spies and difficulty of spotting these. International hotels probably patronised by Germans.

ii.   Pensions. Regulations, less watched by police and spies easier to spot, but gossiping boarders. Satisfactory if owners are reliable.

iii. Lodgings. Regulations. Solitude and unlikelihood of surveillance, but you may be conspicuous and the landlady curious.

Hard to find, but satisfactory if the landlady is sympathetic.

iv.   Staying with friends. Quite satisfactory. You may have to take the family into your confidence. They must not be suspect.

v.   House or flat. Regulations. Flat better than house, where a newcomer living alone arouses curiosity. Devices for taking it in friend's name.

vi.   Charitable Institutions. On no account to be used; strictly supervised and liable to mass arrests.

vii. Brothel. Possible for one night in an emergency, but strict supervision and possible informers.

viii. Prostitute with flat. Possible in an emergency. Prostitutes are supervised as a class and may be used as informers.

Do not stay in any one place long.

Owner of safe house does not necessarily know that you are a subversive agent.

(b)   Prohibited Areas and overcrowded towns. Residence forbidden or subject to special regulations. Evacuation.

(c)   Prohibited persons. Special regulations for Jews, foreigners; Poles in certain parts of Poland.

C.   MOVEMENT.

(a)   Pure locomotion. Regulations for and controls on.

i.   "Neutral zone".

ii.   Prohibited Areas.

iii. Protected places and places put out of bounds for various reasons.

iv.   Certain classes - foreigners, Jews.

Advice for student's country. Also general advice:

i.   Move by day and stick to roads, unless circumstances require you to move by stealth (e.g. in prohibited zone).

ii.   Do not move in a group of more than two.

iii. At night if you meet a motor car or a bicycle, hide.

iv.   Beware of curfew (see later) and dusk hour. Move at rush hours.

v.   Be careful on market-days, or if there has been trouble.

vi.   Crossing of frontiers and demarcation lines and landing from sea.

Controls not always exactly on frontier.

Danger of crossing frontier twice.

Caution about guides.

By-pass town of destination and enter it from inland.

(b)   Trains. Regulations, for security and to prevent overcrowding. Where controlled. Advice for student's country. Also general:

i.   Break up journey.

ii.   In large station routine controls and secret surveillance are likely; in small station you may be noticed and remembered.

iii. Book to the nearest large station. Do not necessarily get out there.

iv. In case train is controlled, it is useful to go in central compartment, on side furthest from corridor.

v. Be as well dressed as possible.

(c) Public Transport. Buses, trams, metro.

(d) Hackney carriages. Taxis, cabs, velo-taxis, tandems.

(e) Motor cars and cycles. Regulations. Difficulty of obtaining. Petrol and tyres.

(f) Cycles. Regulations. Difficulty of obtaining. Convenient but suspected. Special curfew for cyclists.

(g) Shipping (including inland waterways and ferries) and sea-fishing.

D. CURFEW.

Varies from place to place and month to month. Imposed as penalty. Special curfews for traffic, cyclists, young persons.

Exemptions.

E. TRANSPORT OF GOODS.

In trains, in vehicles, on foot.

Regulations, controls and adviceas to transport of incriminating material. Camouflage. Possibility of disowning. Use of Outsider.

F. RATIONS.

Regulations and controls:-

(a) Ration-cards.

(b) Regulations in restaurants etc.

(c) Control of harvesting, slaughtering, fresh-water fishing, fruit-picking, and black market.

(d) How to get food and other commodities.

G. LABOUR.

(a) Conscription.

(b) Control of employment.

H. COMMUNICATIONS. Will be dealt with later.

I. CURRENCY.

Regulations regarding foreign currency and payments in or possession of national currency.

J. ARMS. Death penalty.

K. WIRELESS. Regulations on listening.

L. PUBLICATIONS. Censorship, including advertisements.

M. ALLIED LEAFLETS. To be handed to police at once.

N. AIR RAIDS.

O. BLACK-OUT, including torches.

P. CAMERAS, FIELD-GLASSES, MAPS, SKETCHING - forbidden in certain areas.

Q. TYPEWRITERS. Registered in some countries (or leave this to A. 17).

R. SALVAGE. Paper must not be destroyed in France.

S. ASSEMBLIES. Groups in public; clubs, dancing.

T. PATRIOTIC SYMBOLS, SONGS, etc.

U. JEWS. Sum up their disabilities.

V. POSSIBLE D-DAY RESTRICTIONS. (here or in A. 15).

4. DETECTIVE MEASURES.

A. General Controls, permanent or snap, and raids.

(a) Object.

i. Check of identity.

ii. Enforcement of regulations, e.g. black-market, travel, curfew, labour, arms.

iii.Search for parachutists and other "wanted" men.

iv. "   " Allied airmen.

v. "   " escaped P.O.W.

vi. "   " German deserters.

vii."   " Jews.

Will check papers question, search persons, belongings, and premises.

N.B. Plain-clothes men who compel would-be dodger to go through controls.

(b) Dangerous places.

i. Frontiers and demarcation-lines.

ii. Trains,

iii. Large railway stations.

iv. Paris metro.

v. Cinemas.

vi. Cafes, hotels, restaurants.

vii. Public gatherings.

viii. Bridges and other V.Ps.

(c) Dangerous Times

i. Market days.

ii. Week-ends.

iii. Just before and after curfew.

iv. After disturbances or when wanted men or R.A.F. crews are at large.

v. At times of visits of distinguished persons.

vi. When trains of workers leave for Germany.

vii. When troop trains leave for Eastern front.

viii. National feast days.

ix. When invasion is expected.

Therefore keep alert, have good informant service; conceal incriminating articles; have plausible cover-story prepared in advance; approach policeman with a question.

B. Informers.

Largely looking out for minor offences (black market, illegal listening etc.) Also unconscious informers; therefore regard everybody as a potential informer.

C. Agents Provocateurs. Sometimes after small fry (black marketeers etc.) More dangerous ones provoke subversive talk (by violent Nazism as well as by pretended patriotism); offer services; pose as members of subversive organisation; ask for help as R.A.F. pilots, escapers, etc; trap friendly police who let them pass control with arms; bogus clandestine newspapers.

Note:- Agents who have been released after arrest.

A special form of provocation is to spread a rumour of an Allied landing, which causes patriots to come into the open.

D. Penetration. Double agents. Discretion needed in recruiting men and in contacting other organisations. Double agent may work well for an organisation for a long time before any arrests are made.

E. Surveillance. Spies watch whole community on chance of picking up something; or shadow particular suspect person or place. Certain times and places are especially dangerous - cf. A(b) and (c) above.

F. Direction finding. Will be discussed later.

G. Censorship, open (random) and secret.

Will be discussed later.

H. Interrogation. Already discussed.

I. Black Lists.

(a) of certain classes - Jews, Communists, Freemasons, certain political parties, and groups likely to be anti-German. Drawn up with help of local Nazis and others.

(b)   of particular suspects. Based on all the above sources of information.

Widely circulated and card-indexed. There is, however, some delay in circulating, and C.E. services do not always pass names on to each other.

J.   Mass Arrests - of men likely to be troublesome. Useful for supplying hostages and also made in the hope of catching some big fish in the net. Largely based on black lists.

In some cases men of certain groups are not arrested, but compelled to report regularly.

5. REPRISALS AND BRIBERY.

(a)   Reprisals.

(i)   Shooting hostages already arrested or selected. Threat to go on shooting till wanted man is surrendered.

(ii) Arbitrary arrests and shootings among the population in general.

(iii) Punishment of whole community - curfew, burning and bombing of towns, fines requisitions.

(iv) Punishment of individuals, e.g. family of escaper.

(b)   Population as a screen.

(i)   Local citizens compelled to guard V.P.s and made responsible for sabotage.

(ii) Local citizens placed in position where sabotage will endanger them - e.g. on troop trains.

(c)   Rewards. Given to whole communities for good behaviour - e.g. extra rations, lifting of curfew, release of local P.O.W. after Dieppe raid.

Reprisals vary greatly in intensity according to place and time. Often Germans do not wish by reprisals to advertise successful subversive activity.

A.11
January 1944

SURVEILLANCE.

A. INTRODUCTION.

Surveillance is the keeping of someone under observation without his knowledge.

You are most interested in this question from the Defensive point of view (i.e. knowing what to do about being watched yourself), but a study of the Active aspect (i.e. how to carry out surveillance) is also useful because:-

i. You may want to observe someone secretly yourself.

ii. You will understand better what you are up against.

B. HOW TO CARRY OUT SURVEILLANCE.

The following methods are used by police watchers. If you have to do any surveillance, make use of those methods as far as practicable.

1. Organisation.

a). Best type of watcher.

i. Below average height; no striking peculiarities.

ii. Possessing detailed knowledge of district.

b). Use of team.

i. Police usually employ more than one watcher simultaneously, including women.

ii. A relay system is often organised whereby any watcher who is detected by the quarry is replaced by another.

c). Use of vehicles. Bicycles, private cars and vans are sometimes used.

2. Preparations by watcher.

a). Instructions. The watcher must understand exactly what he has to do, what activities of the quarry are of particular interest, and whether he is to continue watching if detected.

b). Information. The watcher requires all available information about the quarry (description, addresses, usual movements, habits, interests) so as to anticipate the quarry's actions or pick him up again if lost.

c). Equipment.

i. Clothes. These should either fit the locality (e.g. seaman's jersey near docks) or be inconspicuous by their neutrality. In any case, they should be dark rather than light in colour. It is advisable to anticipate any change in the weather. It is sometimes very useful to change all or some clothes en route.

ii. Quiet shoes.

iii. It is unwise to carry any conspicuous article (e.g. stick, large parcel).

iv. Money. It is necessary to take sufficient money, particularly small change.

v. Reading matter often comes in useful during a long period of waiting.

46

vi. Food and tobacco. It may be impossible to obtain those while carrying out surveillance.

vii.Watch, pencil and paper.

d). Cover. The watcher must consider what is to be his cover background and alibi while carrying out surveillance. It is advisable to prepare this beforehand, though he must also be ready to adapt it to any special circum¬stances that may arise.

N.B:- Usefulness of women to provide cover.

e). Plan. If the watcher is one of a team, a plan must be prepared. In particular, visual signals should be arranged (e.g. signal indicating "I have lost quarry").

f). Lavatory. Before starting surveillance, the watcher should relieve himself. (cf. Duke of Wellington).

Technique. (Illustrate with diagrams.)

a). Position of watchers. The distance between the watchers and the quarry should vary according to the circumstances. It is often better to use the opposite side of the road. With a team of watchers, it is useful to change positions occasionally (e.g. when turning corner). Watchers should try to approach the quarry from different angles - not always from behind. With a team, it may be useful for one watcher occasionally to be in front of the quarry. There is no reason why a watcher should not make up distance rapidly by hurrying, provided that he is out of sight of the quarry, and shows some pretext (e.g. looking at his watch).

b). Concealment and camouflage on the move. The watcher should always try to keep something between him and the quarry (e.g. lamp-post, pedestrian). He should mix with other people, walk alongside them, cross the road in company. If the quarry stops or turns back the watcher should not hesitate but should do something definite (e.g. go into shop, speak to passer-by, go straight on).

c). Concealment and camouflage when stationary. The watcher should choose a good place for his station e.g. physically concealed, or as one of a crowd, or in a normal waiting place (e.g. bus stop).

d). Looking at quarry. As soon as the watcher has picked up his quarry, he should note the features by which he intends to recognise him in future. (Those may well be different from the features given in a description.) As far as possible, he should look at the quarry indirectly, making use of shop window reflections, etc. Above all, he must avoid catching the eye of the quarry.

e). Anticipating his movements. The watcher should always try to be one jump ahead of the quarry. In this he will be helped by his knowledge of the district and of the quarry's habits.

f). In a big building. If the quarry enters a big building with more than one exit, it is usually necessary for one watcher to follow him in, unless it is possible for all the exits to be kept under observation.

g). In public vehicles. If the quarry gets on a public vehicle the watcher should try to put himself in such a position that he will be able to hear the quarry's destination before he gets his own ticket. Sometimes it is possible to get on the same vehicle at a later stop, or previous stop.

h). Inside a bar, etc. The watcher should choose his position very carefully so that he can keep the quarry under observation without being watched himself. If he wishes to look directly at the quarry, he should choose a moment when he can look at him naturally (e.g. when drinking). It is always advisable to pay the bill early, and it is usually better to leave the place before the quarry.

C. HOW TO DEFEND yourself against surveillance.

1. Routine Precautions. Whenever you are going anywhere on secret work, you must automatically take routine precautions which will make it difficult for you to be secretly watched.

a). You should always be on the alert to notice strangers hanging about, especially when you are leaving any house.

b). Do not go straight to your destination.

c). Make use of a vehicle, either public or private. If you use the former, board it on the run. If you use the latter, do not take one which offers to pick you up, and start by telling the driver the wrong destination. You should never take a vehicle right up to your destination, but complete the journey on foot.

d). Make some innocent visits on the way.

e). Visit at least one crowded place.

f). Do not walk or hang about in places where you could easily be watched without detecting it.

2. If you suspect that you are being watched.

a). Show no signs of suspicion. Do not quicken your pace and do not look round unnecessarily.

b). Postpone your immediate job; avoid making contact with other agents (use of danger signal).

c). Check up to make sure that you are really being watched and to get the description of the watcher or watchers. It is essential to do this because you may easily imagine that you are being watched, especially if your nerves are strained. The following methods may be used:-

i. Find some pretext to look round (e.g. cross road, do up shoe, light pipe, watch pretty girl).

49

ii. Isolate the watcher from the crowd by going into an empty street or shop.

iii.Surprise the watcher and make him betray his surprise by some quick movement - e. g. jumping on bus, changing direction, stopping round a corner (all with a good pretext).

N.B:- Remember that there may be more than one watcher; do not be satisfied with detecting only one.

3. After making sure that you are being watched. If you have checked up and obtained some sort of a description of your watchers, you have two alternatives open to you:-

a). If it is essential for you to give an appearance of innocence and if you can postpone your immediate job, it is wisest to do so and to behave perfectly innocently. If at the same time you make contact with a number of people, visit shops etc., you will give the police some "clues" to follow up which, when proved false, may convince them of your innocence.

b). If, on the other hand, you must carry out your secret work, you must first shake off the watchers. If there is more than one, you may have to do this piecemeal. You can nearly always drop all but one by taking a vehicle unexpectedly.

The best method for shaking off one watcher in a natural manner is to lead him through a long deserted street or space (where he must remain at a distance) and then to plunge into a crowd or take other sudden action before he has time to catch you up.

In any town where you are going to work you should plan a number of alternative methods for shaking watcher off, so that, if you find yourself under surveillance you will be able to act without hesitation.

4. Subsequent action. If you are under surveillance, you must at once warn all your contacts. It may be necessary for you to

make a get-away at once, If, however, you are not convinced
of the danger, it; may be advisable to have yourself watched
by a colleague, who will easily identify anyone else who is
watching you.

D. CONCLUSION.

If you are being watched it is essential for you to be aware
of it.

1. This will enable you to retain the initiative yourself and
determine your own course of action.

2. It will also give you early warning that you are suspected
(presumably by the police) and enable you to make a get-away
before they are ready to arrest you.

USE OF PREMISES.

1. INTRODUCTION.

It must be recognised that the use of premises must bring with
it special security problems. Normally, premises should be used
for subversive activity as little as possible. The organiser
should try to keep his plans and records in his head and meet
agents in many different places. As the organisation grows, it
will become necessary to use premises for the above purposes.

2. CHOOSING PREMISES.

Field of choice will depend much on the particular country
or region. In thinly populated country districts there may be
opportunities for using isolated buildings - e.g. hiking or ski-
ing huts. In a densely populated country a private house, flat

or commercial establishment in a town may have to be used. In
selecting the latter, the following factors should be considered.

(a) Location.

It is important that strangers may be able to find their way
without arousing suspicion by making enquiries or by their
appearance being out of tune with the district, e.g. a poorly
dressed person will not necessarily be conspicuous in a
wealthy quarter, whereas the converse is not true.

(b) Cover.

i. For the establishment.

Wherever possible an attempt should be made to utilise
an existing concern; any new business is very likely to
be suspect and subject to enquiry. (see below). The usual
office hours should be kept, bills paid normally and genuine
business conducted.

It must fit into the background – e.g. if it is a shop it must
be of the appropriate class for the district.

Its cover must be built up. If possible, genuine business
should be carried on before subversive activity is started.

ii. For visitors.

It must provide cover for agents who come to visit it –
suitable cover both for regular cut-outs and for irregular
visitors or complete strangers – e.g. from abroad. Visitors
must have "genuine" reason for coming.

(c) Control of Access.

There are three degrees of access available in a town; each
degree giving you cover in inverse proportion to the degree
of security.

Examples.

i. A "general" shop, where it is impossible to prevent the entry of police spies. Good cover for establishment and for visitors, very little control of access.

ii. An establishment with individual attention for the clients - e.g. tailor, doctor, dentist. Good cover for establishment, more difficult for visitors, more control of access.

iii.A private office confined to a specific group of clients. Most difficult for police infiltration (need for an adequate story, waiting-rooms etc.). Safes and records may also be kept here. The owner can combine the functions of H.Q. and cut-out, acting as a representative of the organiser, or as a "dummy" organiser. Good cover for establishment, cover for some agents may be difficult, good control of access.

iv. Private residence. Where the occupant has legal cover this may be good, but frequent visits may be dangerous - neighbours may talk, concierge may be informer.

(d) Defensive Facilities.

Consider the suitability of the premises from a defensive point of view - i.e.

i. Facilities for concealing documents and material - e.g. thickness of walls etc.

ii. Facilities for escape (alternative exits). Consider possibility of taking the house or flat next door as a means of escape.

iii.Vulnerability to surveillance.

3. SECURITY PRECAUTIONS.

As many as possible of the following precautions should be taken in connection with any premises, including agent's own place of residence.

(a) The organiser must not use his place of residence and/or his place of occupation for subversive activity.

(b) It is better to recruit the owner or occupant of an existing establishment than to set up a new establishment and instal new personnel. (Give regulations existing in particular country concerning opening of new establishment.) If new premises are being sought, care should be taken not to betray the use to which they are to be put, e.g. indiscreet enquiries about electric current or number of doors.

(c) The principle of dispersal is most important. It is a great mistake to concentrate too many activities in one place – e.g. do not keep your documents at a place where agents meet.

(d) No particular set of premises should be known to more than the necessary minimum number of agents.

(e) Agent must always be able to tell whether a room has been entered and searched during his absence. The best precaution is tidiness, though traps may be set providing they are not conspicuous, e.g. fluff or ash in book, zip fastener on case, blotting paper on pad.

(f) As little incriminating material as possible should be kept on the premises. Anything no longer needed should be destroyed – e.g. code workings. Danger of leaving unfinished code work.

N. B. Traces on blotting paper and writing blocks, carbons and typewriter ribbons.

(g) Hiding places should be prepared. It may be necessary to have both permanent and emergency hiding places – the latter only to be used if the premises are raided while the

incriminating articles are in use. Quantities of arms and
explosives should be put in special caches.

Fireplaces, and any other places in current fashion with the
police, should be avoided. (In this connection, information
about any successful police searches is most valuable.)

Permanent hiding places should be difficult of access rather
than subtle - e.g. burial.

Documents should not be concealed in places where bulky material
might be found - in case they are looking for food, for example.

(h) Preparations should be made for destroying incriminating
evidence which is too dangerous to conceal.

N. B. Quantities of paper burn very slowly, even when petrol-
soaked, and ashes may be deciphered unless broken up.

(i) Provision should be made for persons to escape in case
of sudden danger (alternative exit), and to clear away all
traces. A final check should be made, preferably by someone
who has not helped to clear up.

(j) If cover permits, someone should always be on guard.
It may be very useful (particularly in the case of rooms
situated in a large block) if someone - e.g. the hall-porter
- can be enrolled to act as guard, and a warning system of
communications arranged, though remember danger of informers
among concierges.

(k) All-clear and danger signs should be pre-arranged. These
should be, if possible, visible from outside. If not, method
of arranging room or opening conversation. A "normal" sign
should be used to denote danger. Possibility of limiting times
for calling and only showing sign then.

(l) A constant watch should be kept to see whether the premises are under observation; and when anyone enters or leaves, a check should be made to see that he is not followed, and, if he is, a warning should be arranged.

(m) It may be wise for frequent visitors to alter their dress slightly and arrive by different methods in order to avoid attracting attention.

(n) (Emphasise) In case one set of premises comes under suspicion, an alternative set should be ready, with the necessary cover story built up.

(o) (Emphasise) If any person who knows of the premises is arrested, they should be evacuated at least temporarily.

A. 17
May 44

EXTERNAL COMMUNICATIONS.

INTRODUCTION.

Wireless has already been discussed in a separate lecture. But alternative methods must be considered. W/T is not a suitable medium for long messages, and for various reasons (or accidents) an agent may find himself without W/T communications.

In considering alternative methods, there are two phases to bear in mind, viz:-

a) Present-day conditions, when most of the normal life and communications of the country are functioning.

b) Invasion or battle conditions, when railways and posts will probably not be functioning for civilian use, neutral frontiers may be closed, etc. As the hour of invasion approaches the enemy is certain to put every obstacle in the way of clandestine communication with agents in the field.

Organisations will have to prepare for this by having as many means as possible available.

Therefore consider:-

1.   a) POST.

Letters are written to an accommodation address in a neutral country. The neutral recipient should not know the real purpose of the letter, and may think it a communication from an innocent person to a friend in allied territory. The recipient is not liable for serious penalties for complicity. Nevertheless, as external censorship is strict, for his own protection, and to ensure quick delivery, the sender should remember the following points:-

i.   Apparent innocence and inconspicuousness of the letter are even more essential than for internal mail.

ii.   Writer's name and address should be concealed (Cf. Letters for Internal Delivery). Where letters for abroad must be presented open at the Post Office and sender identify himself, consider use of cut-out.

iii.   All regulations should be complied with in order to avoid delay or destruction of letter.

N.B. It is found that post-cards are more reliable and more quickly delivered than ordinary letters.

Disadvantage of mail is that in times of crisis e.g. D-day, all external post may be stopped or letters destroyed.

b)   TELEGRAMS AND TELEPHONES.

Limited use is made of telegrams with pre-arranged code or crack signal.

Telephone is dangerous and usually impossible.

2. COURIER SERVICE.

It is a useful means of sending certain types of message, e.g. routine reports, any urgently required plans, documents and material which cannot be sent by W/T.

Courier lines from occupied to neutral countries are already established and, where necessary, organisations are put in touch with them.

Method of conveying messages as far as the frontier is identical with that for internal courier services, except that more relays are required.

For crossing the frontier various methods are available.

i. A courier with lawful cover, e.g. business man, diplomat, transport, employee, farmer, or workman with frontier pass, etc.

ii. A courier without lawful cover, e.g. a smuggler.

iii. A "dead" courier. Here the message is concealed on a train or vehicle crossing the frontier and retrieved by a member of the organisation on the far side. (cf. Use of "dead" courier for internal communications).

N.B. Messages are sometimes carried by agents going to or leaving the field.

Disadvantage of a courier service is that travel, particularly across frontiers, is likely to be severely curtailed or prohibited in times of crisis, e. g. D-day.

3. WIRELESS TELEPHONIC COMMUNICATION.

At the request of an organiser in the field a member of his section may be sent over by plane or motor boat to talk to him by wireless telephone. Special training is required for the setting up and use of the apparatus. Where necessary organisations are supplied with a person competent to carry out this sort of communication.

Such a form of communication can only be used on very rare occasions because,

a) it requires to be carefully arranged in advance and a certain amount of notice must be given,

b) it endangers the aeroplane and its crew,

c) the danger to the agent on the ground is obvious.

An additional disadvantage of this form of communication is that in times of crisis, e.g. D-day, the danger to motor boats and single aircraft may be greatly increased and movement at night, particularly in coastal areas, very difficult indeed. Furthermore, the organisation of such conversations would be increasingly difficult.

4. CARRIER PIGEONS AND PHOTOGRAPHY.

Pigeons offer a very useful alternative method of communication; in conjunction with miniature or micro-photography very long messages can be sent by a single bird.

a) Photography.

A pigeon can easily carry a spool of 35 mm. film, containing 36 "frames" or exposures, each about the size of two postage stamps. On each frame it is possible to photograph from one to sixteen pages of foolscap typewriting. If micro-photographic methods are resorted to, a whole issue of Bradshaw could be reproduced and sent by a single pigeon.

b) Pigeons.

The advantages of pigeons are:-

i.   They function independently of other conditions (e.g. trains, posts, etc.) and are therefore unaffected by temporary chaos.

ii.   They cannot be direction found.

iii. If proper measures are taken, it should be very difficult to spot the release of a bird at dawn from, say, a farm in the country.

The disadvantages are:-

i.   They are forbidden and therefore special security measures must be adopted.

ii.   The pigeon has its enemies - e.g. cats and rats in captivity, falcons and farmers with shotguns while on the wing.

iii. They cannot fly during fog or darkness, and bad weather will greatly reduce their speed.

iv.   Delivery can only be made in limited quantities every moon period, so that during the last week of the period pigeons may not be available. Furthermore, supplies may be held up owing to failure of delivery.

A few facts about carrier pigeons:-

i.   They fly at 40/60 m.p.h., but only by daylight. If they are benighted, they will perch and continue the journey at first light.

ii.   A fairly safe all-the-year-round radius is 300 miles; this can be greatly extended during the early summer.

iii. They can be kept in a container for three or four days, and loose in an attic or shed at least fourteen days. (This can be extended to three, and even four, weeks with proper care.)

iv. They need to be fed and watered twice a day and also a certain amount of knowledge of handling is required.

5. B.B.C.

Messages from this country are sent as crack signals in the programme of the country where the recipient is working. The advantage of this method is that it is impossible to ascertain for whom the message is intended.

The disadvantages are as follows:-

a) Replies cannot be sent by the same means.

b) In times of crisis e.g. D-day electric current may be cut off or W/T sets confiscated.

c) Listening in to foreign broadcasts is illegal and the law may become more severely enforced.

d) Sets in occupied countries are wearing out and cannot be replaced.

N.B. In order to overcome these difficulties, special midget receiving sets are now being supplied.

6. ADVERTISEMENTS IN THE PRESS.

Are sometimes used as a means of communication abroad. (Cf. Internal Communications). Newspapers published in occupied territory are received in neutral countries shortly afterwards and can be delivered in Great Britain a few days later. Advertisements published therein can be used as crack signals to indicate a safe arrival or that certain events have taken, or are about to take place.

The disadvantage of this means of communication is that in times of crisis the export of newspapers from occupied to

neutral countries may be greatly curtailed or prohibited. In
any case, the publication of advertisements is likely to be
much delayed.

7. GENERAL PRECAUTIONS.

For external messages the same precautions must be taken as
for internal. Particularly dangerous is the risk that, as a
result of penetration, the enemy will send false messages from
the field. Signs should be arranged to prove that messages are
genuine.

A. 19

August 44

THE CELL SYSTEM.

For many types of subversive activity - e.g. propaganda,
passive resistance, etc. - and with all large organisations,
it is necessary to organise on a basis of cells; this
strengthens security.

1. DEFINITION.

A cell is a small group working subversively inside some
existing group of individuals - e.g. factory, party, railway
workers, group workers going into Germany.

The principle is the same as that for the sections, the
differences being that a section is a subversive group within
a large subversive group or organisation.

2. EXPANSION.

i. One of the most important functions of a cell is to recruit
other cells. Best method is for one member of each cell to
have duty of recruiting a man outside who will organise

another cell. Similarly, another man in new cell will recruit a further cell, and so on.

ii. As recruiter in first cell is only man to have contact with organiser of second cell, security is maintained to the highest degree. Value of this is that in the event of one agent coming under suspicion, police will take a long time to trace others, and even if part of the organisation is discovered it does not necessarily reveal the whole.

iii. An alternative method is by radiation, whereby the members of a cell recruit the organisers of more than one new cell. Quicker expansion and more direct communication, but security reduced.

iv. Chain system most suitable for simple activities not requiring complicated orders or exact timing - e.g. "passive resistance"; radiation system best where speed and co-ordination are essential - e.g. secret armies.

3. CONTROL.

i. Policy must be laid down from the top and carried out uniformly throughout organisation.

ii. No cell is superior to others; orders are simply passed on from above.

iii. Field of recruitment for each chain of cells should be limited - e.g. one department in a factory - so that each group of cells is kept separate from others and under control of agent appointed to look after it.

iv. The organiser should limit the number of cells to be formed in each department or group. The cell members will be the "shock troops", influencing outsiders to undertake subversive action also.

4. INTERNAL WORKING

i. Number.

A cell should contain only a small number of individuals (three to eight).

ii. Distribution of Functions.

The cell as a whole will have a special function according to the general policy from above, but each member can also have a special function. Here is a possible lay-out for a cell of five members:-

a. Chief of Cell - responsible for liaison.

b. Security of the cell - though each member is responsible for reporting immediately any suspicious incident, e.g. absence of a cell member from work.

c. Information - perhaps on orders from above, information on a specific target is wanted - All cell members might contribute, No. 3 collate before passing on to chief.

d. Material - if active operations are planned.

e. Liaison down to next cell.

5. PLANS FOR EMERGENCY.

Plans must be laid in advance for the possibility of a break in a chain of cells which would leave some cells isolated.

Possibilities are:

i. General directives on the policy to be pursued in that eventuality.

ii. The linking of the last cell in the chain with the organiser of the whole chain, thus making it circular.

iii. Emergency address - e.g. to appear in an advertisement in an agreed paper, or boite-aux-lettres.

6. CONCLUSION.

i.   The cell system has obvious disadvantages - viz. slowness, inefficiency, remote control.

ii.   Nevertheless, it is the only system of large-scale organisation that affords the necessary degree of security.

iii.   It is particularly suitable for a continuous campaign of simple activities - e.g. propaganda, passive resistance, minor sabotage, strikes - and also for ground work preparatory to an armed revolt. It may also be used for penetrating existing organisations and influencing their policy and activities.

A.20

August 44

SECURITY OF ORGANISATION.

1. INTRODUCTION.

The security of the organisation as a whole depends on the security of individual agents. The principles set out in the lecture should be learnt by every member of the organisation, and particular care should be taken to ensure that recruits know them, understand them, and understand the reason behind each one.

2. SECURITY STANDING ORDERS.

i.   No member will be told more about the organisation than is necessary for him to do his job.

ii.   No member will attempt to find out more about the organisation than he is told.

iii. Each member will have a specific job or jobs and will not undertake any other without orders.

N.B. Danger of over-enthusiastic or lonely agent wanting to do too much work, work for which he is not suited, or work which will bring him into contact with too many people.

iv. Members must only use service names of all other members.

v. No member will recognise another member in public for other than duty purposes unless they are supposed to know each other in everyday life.

vi. No member will make a recruit or contact another organisation unless ordered to do so.

vii. No member will carry arms unless a cover story is impossible, e.g. during wireless transmission or receptions. Where an agent carries a weapon he must be ready to use it.

viii. Every member will make a daily search of his room, clothes and effects to ensure that he has nothing compromising which can be found.

ix. Every member is responsible for ensuring at all times that he is not followed.

x. Every member will report anything suspicious at once. If he thinks he is suspect himself he must ensure that in so doing he does not bring suspicion on another.

xi. Safety signals will be arranged for all meetings. Danger should always be indicated by something normal, generally the absence of a safety signal.

xii. Strict punctuality will be observed for all meetings.

xiii. Not more than two agents will normally meet at the same time.

xiv. Passwords and countersigns will be given exactly as
arranged and no variations accepted.

xv. For every journey, meeting, or conversation a simple
cover story will be prepared in advance.

xvi. Every member must know what to do in case of emergency.
(see below.)

3. EMERGENCY ACTION.

A. Organisers.

Organisers must so far as possible have plans ready for an
emergency. The essential thing in an emergency is to act quickly,
as there is often little or no time to plan when the occasion
arises. The organiser must consider the following points:

a. Decide what contacts, plans and places are affected;

b. Warn the contacts to take their pre-arranged measures;

c. Postpone or drop any activities that are affected;

d. Clean up any places that are affected - i.e. destroy or
conceal material and documents, cease to use R.V.'s;

e. Possibly send a message to H.Q. in this country;

f. If an agent has been arrested, find out the reason for
his arrest and whether he has talked.

g. Help the arrested agent to escape if it can be done
without prejudicing the security of the organisation.

B. Other Agents.

Each member of the organisation should know the following:

a. what warning signals will be used;

b. what other members he must warn himself;

c. where to go (hide-out, cover story etc.);

d. what contacts and activities he must drop;

e. how to re-establish contact.

N.B. i. This will not always preclude the necessity of giving him further orders when the emergency arises.

ii. Where an agent is put in contact with an escape line he must be told that he will strictly adhere to all instructions given by members of that line.

4. CONCLUSION.

Security is essential for the existence of a clandestine organisation and all responsible members of the organisation should constantly be on the lookout for breaches of the above rules, which should never go unnoticed and should always be brought to the notice of the offender.

B. 3

June 1943

SELECTION OF DROPPING POINTS AND ARRANGEMENTS FOR THE RECEPTION OF AGENTS AND STORES BY AIR.

INTRODUCTION.

Agents who are going into the field must know how Dropping points are selected and what are the limitations on choice of area on account of technical, topographical and weather considerations.

Agents should also understand the air point of view as regards both the safety of the carrying aircraft and the difficulty of location and recognition of a particular area by night.

TECHNICAL CONSIDERATIONS ETC.

1. A good Dropping Point should be:

a. An open space not less than 400 ms. square, and, if possible, 800 square.

b. Of a smooth and level surface, if persons are to be dropped.

c. On uncultivated ground, so as to avoid evidence in the form of foot marks etc.

d. Soft but not swampy ground.

e. Free from all wires or high-tension cables in the vicinity.

f. Free of all trees without trees of any size surrounding the area which might obscure the aircraft's view of the lights. Turning circle of aircraft some 4 miles in diameter, and lights must be visible all the time.

g. Away from sharply rising ground (hills of 100 m.). Hills of more than 300 m. should be 10 miles away for night dropping. For these reasons valleys are unsuitable unless several miles wide. The aircraft requires to increase speed from 225 k.p.h. up to 290 k.p.h. to climb. This would take several miles.

h. Near some cover for concealment of personnel and equipment.

2. Weather must be favourable. Usually bright moonlight. Average night available: five or six on either side of full moon, making eleven or thirteen in all. Operation can, in favourable circumstances, be carried out without moon, but some very reliable landmark, such as a large lake, is

necessary. Operation will take place on first night of
favourable weather when aircraft available.

3. Lighting. Present normal operational system

Three white lights in line, 100 m. between each light; the
downwind light duplicated at a distance of 10 m. by a white
flashing light.

Variations may be agreed for specific operations, and the
white flashing light will give a recognition signal which
will be answered in an agreed manner from the aircraft. Morse
signals by torch must be very slow and distinct. Avoid letters
E, T, H, I, S and V. Lights are turned on immediately the
sound of the aircraft is heard and pointed in that direction,
and the aircraft followed round with the lights kept on
during the whole operation until the signal for the end of
the operation is received. Lights should be pointed about
10° ahead of the direction of the sound so that the pilot may
be looking as directly as possible down the light beam. Care
should be taken to allow, if possible, for deceptive effects
of echoes in the neighbourhood. Practise pointing at sound of
aircraft by day with eyes shut.

4. Drift. Parachutes are released at a height of 500 feet
(160–170 m.), and the average drift may be taken as 60 m.
down-wind for every 5 m.p.h. of wind-speed. (The highest
wind-speed safe for operations is 20 m.p.h.) Reception
committee is responsible for placing the lights in such a
manner as to allow for drift. Aircraft will fly along line of
lights against the wind passing first over the white light
and then releasing the parachutes when vertically over the
last red light. Speed of aircraft: lowest of which it is
capable – Halifax about 140 m.p.h. (225 k.p.h.). Strength
of wind may be judged by committee by handkerchief method –
extend handkerchief held by corner when on highest ground in

neighbourhood; if blown just horizontal by the wind, speed is about 15 m.p.h.; if blown out about 45° below horizontal, wind is about 10 m.p.h.

METHOD OF SELECTION.

On very large-scale map of the district - i.e. 1 : 50,000 - with good details; 1 : 75,000 not very serviceable unless with very good details. British Ordnance 1 - i.e. 1 : 63,000 - very good because of great accuracy, bur such high standard of map may not always be available for occupied countries.

Areas are generally selected in the first place by agents in the field. In such cases, locations are reported to England, using the appropriate map reference system; air point of view taken into account by consultation in England; agreement or not reported by radio.

(Note: The systems appropriate to the various Country Sections will be found in - "Map Reading". At the end of the lecture students' knowledge of their appropriate system should be checked by a short test.)

AIR POINT OF VIEW.

The R.A.F. must ensure:

1. The safety of the carrying aircraft.

2. Certainty of recognition of correct area.

1. The Safety of the Carrying Aircraft.

To ensure this, they must avoid.

a. Heavily defended areas.

b. Enemy aerodromes.

c. Sharply rising ground, when flying low.

71

They must also be sure that the aircraft will be clear of
enemy-occupied territory during the hours of darkness. This
last consideration limits operations to distant countries
during summer months.

2. Certainty of Recognition of Correct Area.

To ensure this, the R.A.F. must rely on map-reading as well
as on navigational instruments. When taking position by map-
reading, the aircraft will fly at between 500 and 1,000 m.
thus running a great risk if vicinity of heavily defended
areas and enemy aerodromes has not been avoided. The following
aids for fixing position on the map are used as landmarks:

a. Coast-line.

b. Rivers and canals. Ideal Width: 50 m.; if narrower, should
not be tree-lined.

c. Large lakes of distinctive shape – at least 800 m. square.

d. Large woods of distinctive shape - at least 800 m. square.
Care must be taken to report such landmarks which differ from
the map as the result of cutting.

e. Straight roads at least 1½k. long – especially the crossing
of two such roads.

f. Railways, especially after snow.

g. Large towns. If outstandingly large, can be distinguished
from any others, but otherwise not reliable. In any event,
very large towns are likely to be heavily defended and must
therefore be avoided.

Water can be very easily seen. A combination of features is
much the best landmark - e.g. a large distinctive lake with a
long, straight road running beside it; or a large, clearly-
shaped wood with a railway nearby.

Some final point of recognition is required that is quite unmistakeable and not more than 10 k. away from the actual area in which the lights are to be displaced. As soon as the aircraft is over the final point of recognition the pilot will turn in the direction of the field and immediately begin looking for the lights.

Church towers and other prominent buildings cannot easily be seen and used as guides - except, perhaps, for direction-marks to be followed during the final run-up.

The paramount importance of choosing an area which can easily be recognised at night from the air will be understood when it is realised that an aircraft circling round searching for the area will most likely arouse the neighbourhood and attract unwelcome attention to the reception committee.

RECEPTION ARRANGEMENTS.

The difficulties of the Reception Committee may be appreciated when it is considered that:

a. The Committee may receive from four to eight, or more, containers, each weighing 300 lbs. (130 kg.).

b. The operation may take place on any one of moon-period nights, notice of which night only being received shortly before the operation. Some operations may take place without a moon, but in any event favourable weather must be awaited.

c. The time spent on the landing-ground after the aircraft has arrived must be reduced to the absolute minimum necessary for the disposal of the containers.

d. At least fourteen days' notice is required in England of an operation and longer notice is very helpful.

The leader's orders for the Reception Committee should embrace the following points:

1. Information. Sufficient to enable the individual members to make their personal arrangement and cover for being present, but no more.

2. Intention: A clear statement of what the leader intends to achieve - i.e. to receive and dispose of so many containers and so many agents.

3. Method.

a. Approach to dropping area and rendezvous. Members should preferably proceed independently or in pairs - not in a large body. Exact directions should be given to appropriate members of the committee as to where they are to take the material assigned to them and when their particular part in the operation will finish.

b. Four men detailed individually to work the lights.

c. A man detailed as responsible for any arms to be brought to the rendezvous, arming of members of the committee for the operation and disposal of these arms afterwards.

d. Lookouts round the area during the operation.

e. Individual members responsible for spotting the parachutes as they descend and going at once to the spot. For this and all other purposes it is advisable to number the members of the Reception Committee, and parachutes should be spotted and marked by numbers, the first to reach the ground being marked by No. 1, the second to reach the ground by No. 2, and so on. Beware of saying the first parachute to leave the plane in the case of containers, as all will appear to be dropped simultaneously, although in reality they are dropped at fraction-of-a-second intervals.

74

f. Someone detailed to make sure no odds and ends have been
left on the landing-ground. The total number of containers
etc. in the operation should be marked on each one.

g. Personal guides for any new agents being dropped. (New
arrivals should be careful not to speak loudly as they will be
deaf from noise of aircraft engine.)

h. Transport arrangements. Availability or otherwise of
transport will govern to a great extent the method of
organisation.

4. Administration.

a. Transport. Lorry or cart with circulation permit.

b. Three red torches and one white torch, plus spares.

c. Sandbags to pack parachutes and odds and ends before
burying. (Any necessary holes would have been dug in advance.
Consider advisability of two alternative burying places 1,000m.
or more apart, both prepared in the case of emergency.)

d. Spades.

e. Snuff or pepper for scattering over places which have been
walked on, or where burying has taken place, to deter dogs.

f. Gloves or cloth if containers to be transported whole, as
handles are thin.

g. If during any part of the transport absolute silence is
vital, then a cloth or other material for muffling containers.

5   Inter-Communication.

a. Password and/or audible challenge and reply.

b. S-phone and Eureka if being used. Note; These latter are operated by trained personnel, and in the case of Eureka the organiser must not override the operator's choice of position unless vital to security.

The Committee should be fully ready the moment the agreed stand-by time arrives, and for security reasons it may be advisable to have the Committee assemble at a rendezvous some little way from the actual area, well beforehand, and the agreed stand-by time only announced when all are assembled at the rendezvous. Opportunity might be taken for technical instruction in arms etc. during time of waiting.

At least some members of the Reception Committee will depend both on the number of people available and on the degree of security necessary in view of the local condition. Four men are required to every one container, but it will probably not be found advisable to have four times the number of men as there are containers expected and groups of four will have to deal with more than one container.

It is advisable to arrange for some constant observation on the security of dropping area, in case of police enquiries or careless talk, both before and after any operation. For this purpose someone living in the locality will be necessary.

Use of two simultaneous or alternative grounds about 3 - 5k. apart has been found an advantage. The pilot is warned to expect lights at both grounds or 1 only.

Last-minute alterations should be avoided unless absolutely essential; otherwise confusion, with consequent danger to all, is bound to result.

Finally, London appreciate any helpful comments agents can send back about operations - e.g. details if any contents damaged by fall, so that items may be better protected in future.

ENEMY FORCES.

1. General.

The aim of these lectures is to present a clear picture of the
forces which oppose the agent, either openly or secretly. By
this means, he ascertains the nature of the opposition, the
degree of danger to be expected, and will have a basis for
planning measures of self-protection.

2. Police and C.E.

He must therefore have a sound understanding of the German
police and C.E. authorities, together with any Nazi Party
organisations and national police which may be used against
him. He must know what kind of work they do, in what way each
is dangerous, and how he may recognise them.

3. Armed Forces.

In addition, if engaged in para-military work, he will require
to be able to identify opposing enemy troops and their weapons.
In any case, for general cover, to show residence in occupied
country, he must have a background knowledge, particularly of
uniforms. Furthermore, by being able to recognise enemy weapons
and uniforms, he will be enabled to send simple non-technical
reports on military intelligence matters.

4. Flexibility - regional treatment.

It is essential that the subject-matter, and emphasis applied
to it, should be adapted to the student's nationality, i.e. -

(a) Western Occupied Countries. - France, Belgium, Holland,

Denmark and Norway. First emphasis should be placed on
German police and C.E. services (Gestapo, S.D., Abwehr,
G.F.P.) and their activity in the individual country
studied. National police play an important role and are
worthy of separate treatment – France taken as an example.
Nazi Party formations only dangerous as accessory police and
para-military services.

(b) German Reich with incorporated territories. – Germany,
Austria, Alsace-Lorraine, incorporated Czechoslovakia and
Poland (General Gouvernement virtually the same).

A full study of the Nazi Party system is here necessary as a
basis for police and C.E.; individual party formations e.g. S.A.
and Civil S.S. must be known in greater detail, The German police
and C.E. are treated as fully as before with the inclusion of
static uniformed police, e.g. Schupo and Gendarmerie.

(c) Eastern territories Balkans and Italy. Again first emphasis
is given to German police and C.E. services, as in (a), with
stress on uniformed mobile formations (Einsatzkommandos). No
separate treatment is given to national police and Quisling
organisations, their role being briefly discussed. Such German
party formations are included, as work in those territories
for specific reasons.

5. Armed Forces Recognition.

Equal importance should be given to arms and equipment on the
one hand and uniforms on the other. These must be explained
and revised throughout pictorially and by models. It is
above all essential to distinguish the different arms of the
service. Detailed organisation of units and formations should
be avoided. Stress is laid on the troops likely to be met with
in the country concerned.

6. Other subjects of general application.

(a) Intelligence Reports. To be ready for such eventualities, the agent must have explained to him what military information is likely to be of interest to the Allies (based on the foregoing recognition), the limitations of his work in this respect, and in what manner he should write and send his message.

(b) German Light Weapons. Not only the recognition but the handling of certain essential German light weapons is to be studied and revised. The agent must be able to use them and to pass on his knowledge.

C. 1 & 2
July 1944

GERMAN COUNTER-ESPIONAGE.

INTRODUCTION

(a) The enemy Forces Course.

The course of twelve lectures falls into two halves:-

1. Enemy police and C.E. forces in Occupied Territory.

2. Enemy armed forces.

Followed by two periods of revision and recognition practice relating to both.

(b) Enemy Police and Counter-Espionage Authorities.

In occupied countries four types of organisation are of importance.

I. German C.E. Authorities who direct and take the initiative in security work. They specialise in the investigation of subversive activity and will normally work in secret; hence usually in plain clothes. They may be civil or military. (C. 1 and 2)

II. German uniformed police, military or civil, for the maintenance of order. They are used for routine control of the civil population, may carry out acts of repression, and do not work clandestinely. (C. 3)

III. National police of the occupied country concerned, either uniformed or plain clothes. This will vary in importance according to the functions and amount of authority left to it, either now or in invasion conditions. (C. 4)

IV. Nazi or pro-Nazi party organisations, German or indigenous. These will play an auxiliary role, either para-military, assisting in maintaining order and in repression; or C.E., acting as informers etc. against resistance groups. (C. 5)

In all these cases three main questions will be examined, which bear directly on the agent's self-protection: -

1. What kind of work do they do?

2. In what particular ways are they important or dangerous to the agent?

3. How may they be recognised?

(c) German C.E. Authorities.

1. Centralised Control.

(i) Several different authorities, civil and military, are occupied in C.E. and general security work. All civil authorities are under one unified command – "Security H. Q." in Berlin (R.S.H.A.). Military security is separately organised under Armed Forces command, but in practice is believed to be falling more and more under the domination of the above H.Q.

(ii) The same unified direction exists in occupied countries where C.E. work amongst the civil population is controlled by a "Security Commander" (B. d. S.). He will also control the work of the plain clothes national police.

2.   Party Domination.

(i)   Nazi Party control is strongly in evidence, especially on a high level since Party men have been appointed to all the more important posts. Owing to recent developments, its presence is likely to be felt in military, as well as in civil authorities.

(ii) In general however German civil rather than military authorities provide the more frequent source of danger for the agent chiefly owing to this political character.

A.   CIVIL SECURITY POLICE

1.   General Composition and Activities.

(a)   Three authorities are concerned

(i)   Geheime Staatspolizei. (Gestapo) - the State Political Police.

(ii) Kriminalpolizei (Kripo) - the State Criminal Police.

These two make up the Sicherheitspolizei (Sipo) proper, i.e. the Security Police of the State.

(iii) Sicherheitsdienst (S.D.) - the Security Service of the Nazi Party. Now directly affiliated to the State Police in organisation and duties.

The whole is usually known as "Sipo and S.D.".

(b)   In occupied territory their work does not fall into

separate spheres. They form one and the same C.E. organisation (Sipo - S.D.) under one leadership.

They therefore co-operate closely and may actually be combined in the same unit.

(e.g. Einsatz-Kommandos - described later.)

(c)   Three distinct types of job, however, necessarily exist, and each is dominated by one of the three authorities;-

(i)   Political investigation and executive work.

This is the field of the Gestapo, but many of its key members are also S.D. men. Criminal police may also assist in investigation.

(ii) Political intelligence service.

This is essentially the field of the S.D., though some information may quite well come via the other two branches.

Those are the principal C.E. Services.

(iii) Criminal Investigation.

i.e. the work of the Kripo which is not directly concerned with C.E.

2.   Importance to the Agent.

(a)   Political bias. This is the essential feature of the Sipo and S.D., i.e. the aim to preserve the Nazi Regime at all costs rather than maintain abstract standards of order and justice. In occupied territory it will, however, seek to destroy any activity directed against a German or Germanised system of administration, military as well as civil.

(b)   S.S. domination. Its close identification with the Nazi Party is shown by the great majority of members drawn from the

S.S., i.e. the "elite" of the Party. So close is this that in each occupied country as in Germany the chief of S.S. is also the chief of the German police. All recruiting is now via the S.S. and recruits pass through S.S. training schools.

(c) Independent authority. Its activities and powers are not subject in any way to the judicial and police system of the country even where this system is still officially in existence. Use is made of "S.S. and police courts" which can deal rapidly with cases of obvious subversive activity according to German police laws and expediency.

(d) Clandestine activities. It works behind the normal facade of uniformed police, German and foreign, watching them as well as any possible suspect.

(e) Civilian agents. In this respect it can make considerable use of political pressure and blackmail. The main types will include:-

Members of Nazi organisations and Nazi sympathisers.

Germans or other nationals, on whose relatives or friends pressure can be exerted.

Released criminals.

Mercenaries, working only for direct material reward.

and may include a minority of:-

Released P.W.s or foreign workers.

Released Allied agents.

Jews, black-marketeers and others who retain their liberty only by working as police agents.

Special gangs are being used (e.g. in France) for the more unsavoury types of C.E. work, e.g. as thugs seizing suspects for the Gestapo, contacts for hotels, brothels etc. as well as general spying for the S.D. They are mobile, subsist largely on the proceeds of private property they have raided and are recruited amongst the lowest social types and criminals (a large proportion of non-Germans).

(f)   Military security. It will not in theory interfere with any purely or primarily military matters in occupied territory, but will have liaison with the military security authorities with whom there has often been friction. In practice there are growing signs that it will interfere with and infiltrate into these. Even where there is a military administration the Sipo and S.D. is supreme in C.E. Work among the civil population.

3.   Recognition.

(a)   For all clandestine and most routine work the Sipo and S.D. will wear civilian clothes. In this case its members could only be identified by their documents.

e.g. (i) Identity disc of Gestapo.

(ii) Sipo and S.D. identity card. (red)

(iii) S.S. membership card (these to be described).

(b)   They may, however, participate in work of a para-military nature, near the front or in areas of large-scale resistance, and there co-operate with uniformed authorities. In this case, they would wear:-

Field grey uniform.

Peaked cap with death's head.

Tunic with black collar patches (plain on right, S.S. rank on left), national eagle on left sleeve, army rank on shoulder.

Open collar with tie.

Sam Browne belt.

SD Black diamond patch on lower left arm bearing "S.D." usually denotes members of this organisation.

(c) All members who belong to the S.S. may wear the black, party uniform of the "General S.S." (death's head on cap, black collar patches as above, swastika arm-band). This is rarely worn in occupied territory.

The above characteristics are common to all the Sipo and S.D., but its three services can be considered separately from the following points of view:-

1. GESTAPO

(a) C.E. WORK

(i) It is the authority devoting its attention most exclusively to C.E. against subversive organisations and influences amongst the civil population.

(ii) It will deal with all crimes or illegal activity having political significance, usually after the national police (sometimes German criminal or military police) has made a first investigation. It will therefore work against both organisations within the country, or foreign agents whose work is now bound up with them.

(iii) It has executive authority, i.e. the power to arrest and punish as well as to investigate. It can make immediate use of protective custody or the concentration camp. Less serious cases may be deported for forced labour in Germany.

(iv) It has two main lines of action in occupied countries:-

Supervision of national police and civil authorities generally (clandestine or otherwise).

Independent investigation work followed by punitive measures. Owing to lack of co-operation with the former the proportion of this work is growing.

(v)   It will have specialist staff for particular problems, e.g. Communists, Jews, workers (German or foreign), movement of Germans abroad, the Press, or any institution with political influence, e.g. the church, teachers, free-masons.

Frontier control is essentially a Gestapo matter and the Frontier Police (Grenzpolizei) is actually part of the "Sipo" though always in uniform (see later). Outside C.E. work, the Gestapo is also concerned in Germany with breaches of economic laws and antisocial conduct like defeatism, grumbling etc.

(vi)   Personnel. It employs greater numbers of people than other security authorities. These are of varying quality and experience.

On the one hand the organising and specialist staff, which includes a high proportion of S.D. men.

On the other the lower ranks whose only qualities are political reliability and lack of scruple.

Members of the criminal police and even of foreign police forces have also been transferred. Women have been recruited in Germany and some work in Occupied Territory.

(vii)   Methods. It makes use of all the detective methods employed by C.E. authorities in general (see A lectures) – either the more routine (surveillance, search, black lists, informant service etc.) or the more subtle (provocation or penetration). There are few cases of real originality in method, but there is no legal restriction on its use of force.

It also makes full use of all the types of agent mentioned above.

(viii) H.Q's Gestapo stations are called in order of importance: - Gestapo-leitstelle; Gestapo-stelle; Aussen-stelle.

(b)   IMPORTANCE TO THE AGENT

Main features and dangers summarised:-

(i)   Its principal motive of political hatred and fear of patriotic resistance, hence violent measures.

(ii)   Its application of all available political power and influence to C.E. work, e.g. it makes use of Party organisations as a source of information; it is always backed by the authority of the S.S.; it can bring pressure on people to work for it; and it is independent of legal control.

(iii)   Its executive powers, enabling it to punish without trial.

(iv)   Its use of large numbers of people, which are an advantage in e.g. surveillance, round-ups and supervision of other authorities.

(v)   Its hold over the imagination of the untrained civilian which has been increased by a skilful use of propaganda and "build up". In his eyes it tends to give its name to all security authorities.

(vi)   N.B. Certain limitations to its power and efficiency. i.e. variable quality of its personnel many of whom lack experience and knowledge of the country concerned; its dependence on the official police as a source of information of which it will be deprived by any refusal to co-operate on the part of the latter; corruption is by no means unknown; it is not by any means exempt from the supervision of the Party S.D.

2.   SICHERHEITSDIENST

(a) WORK

(i) A special and powerful section of the S.S. whose aim is primarily to safeguard the security of the Nazi Party internally and externally, but in practice also that of the State. Its work runs, therefore, closely parallel to that of the Gestapo.

(ii) It works chiefly as a political information service, spying on German and foreigner, Nazi and non-Nazi alike. This information can be put to great use in C.E. work, and there is therefore a close liaison to the Gestapo to whom it will hand over suspects for suitable treatment.

(iii) Its members, who are paid by the Party and include some of its most influential men, may also be members, known or unknown, of any other state authority, especially the police or even of industrial undertakings. Those in the police are often appointed direct from the Party with little or no police training. Some may even belong to the armed forces.

(iv) Since it can hold key positions in the Gestapo, it may also wield executive authority, especially in occupied countries.

(v) The Wehrmacht recognises its authority even in military security work. The armed forces belong so far primarily to the S.D. field of investigation, though the Gestapo may be associated with it in this work.

(vi) It also organises political espionage in neutral countries.

(vii)   It may employ any of the same types of agent used by the Gestapo though they will tend to be fewer and of higher grade.

(viii) H.Q.s S.D. stations in Germany are called in order of importance - Leitabschnitte, Abschnitte, Nebenstellen. In occupied countries they are likely to be combined with Gestapo stations.

(b)   IMPORTANCE TO THE AGENT.

Main features and dangers summarised:-

(i)   A powerful political elite with controlling influence on a high level.

(ii)   Not numerous, but man for man more powerful than members of the Gestapo or other police (outside the S.D.) who must co-operate with them and in general fear them.

(iii)   A dangerous information service with members generally well placed in any sphere of military or civil life; dangerous to Germans and patriots alike.

(iv)   Little heard of because of clandestine methods. In occupied territory it tends to hide in the shadow of the Gestapo and other police. More often than not the identity of its members is unknown. Special danger of penetration by the S.D. of foreign as well as German official organisations. It is willing to wait long periods for this to take effect.

N.B.   Its danger to other subversive organisations in neutral countries.

(v)   Its presence may be suspected amongst any Gestapo personnel doing important investigations. In this case it will wield at least equal authority and do exactly the same job.

(vi)   Likely to be used for more delicate and high-level

89

investigations, e.g. any possible opposition within the army or the Party.

3. KRIMINAL POLIZEI

(a) WORK

The investigation and detection of ordinary civil crime, not of a political nature; i.e. not directly interested in resistance work.

(b) IMPORTANCE TO THE AGENT.

(i) No C.E. work of its own initiative; not believed to be sent to occupied countries in large numbers but:

(ii) It may investigate a crime whose nature is not political at first sight. Moreover it will assist in the pursuit of all missing persons, whether wanted for political reasons or not.

(iii) It may be required to assist the security authorities in an investigation, because of its technical experience, or in supervising controls. Many of its former personnel have in any case been drafted into the Gestapo.

B. MILITARY SECURITY AUTHORITIES

1. ABWEHR - German Intelligence Service

(a) Character and Activities.

(i) General. The Abwehr is the official directing authority in all intelligence matters affecting the Wehrmacht, i.e. offensive espionage and sabotage as well as C.E.

(ii) Command. It is an inter-service organisation working under the High Command (O.K.W.), but in practice its work, especially in C.E., is believed to be falling more and more

under the control of the H.Q. of Sipo and S.D. in Berlin
(R.S.H.A.)

(iii) Scope. It is a world-wide organisation. In peacetime it
can be assumed to have had representatives in all countries
according to strategic importance. Its C.E. staff have
been and still are mainly concentrated in German-occupied
countries, but its channels of information on this subject
will extend to neutral and may extend to Allied countries.

(iv) Personnel. In German-occupied country its staff is
composed of officers of the armed forces – any of the
three services. Relatively small in numbers, they include
experienced and able men, including technical staff most of
whom date from peace time, but personnel recruited in war
time is often not of the same quality. Officers do not hold
very high rank but have an authority extending beyond their
rank. They include Sonderfuhrer or civilians commissioned for
special qualifications.

In neutral countries its staff has, of course, innocent cover,
generally diplomatic or commercial, the latter is probably
the more effective as the former has been much abused. Either
cover may be supplied by other Axis or satellite powers.

(v)   Political Tendencies. The original Abwehr personnel was
not concerned with political matters and owed no particular
allegiance to the Nazi Party. Many of this staff remain, who
are therefore very different in spirit from the Sipo and
S.D. There has been infiltration of personnel from the latter
however, and replacements on a high level. This means greater
Party (especially S.S.) control.

(vi) Civilian agents are used in fairly large numbers and
are of varying quality. In this case there is rarely question
of political enthusiasm or pressure. They normally work for

material gain. Further they are under the complete control of the individual officer who recruits and operates them.

They range from higher diplomatic and social circles, probably penetrated before the war, to low-grade types, without much training, who are expected to collect an indiscriminate array of information.

(vii) Efficiency. Sharing in the initial success of the German armies, its prestige seems to have suffered greatly in the later course of the War. Errors in its intelligence, loose organisation allowing too much individual licence, and failure to sift the information received, were weaknesses resulting in an enquiry (late 43). The resulting purge and the encroachments of the Sipo and S.D. will probably have spurred it to greater efficiency.

(viii) Static H.Q.s

In occupied countries the Abwehr stations are called in order of importance:- Abwehrstelle, Nebenstelle, Aussenstelle.

In neutral countries the clandestine set-up is known as "Kriegs-organisation" and generally centres around members of the legation staff.

(ix) Mobile organisation in areas of military operations.

(likely to be now in use in the west) The above stations are replaced by Abwehr-gruppen, Abwehr-kommandos, or Abwehr-trupps, which follow the main H.Q.s of military formations. They have cover names and their own W/T and motor transport.

(x) In each case three main sections organise:- espionage, sabotage (both material and moral), C.E.

(b) C.E. Work.

(i) General. Protection of the armed forces in occupied

country - their personnel, material and working - against all kinds of subversive activity. Though in certain countries it has carried out C.E. work in protection of civil targets, it is now expected to be restricted to military security.

(ii)　Control of armed-forces security.

Via the military commanders, it will provide security directives for military intelligence officers and will thereby direct the work of the military security police (G.F.P.) with whom it co-operates closely. Abwehr officers are normally attached to these intelligence officers down to Corps H.Q., and there is also liaison between local Abwehr and Divisional H.Q.

(iii)　Independent investigations amongst troops or civilians concerning e.g. detection of enemy agents; serious breaches of security; treachery, desertion or defeatism; carelessness on the part of Wehrmacht or civilians; political agitation and propaganda against troops. It may also have a representative in Gestapo enquiries since the interests of the two may overlap.

(iv)　Specialist personnel in occupied countries are employed in e.g.

Censorship of mail, telephone and publications. W/T security, involving close relations with the Army D/F-ing service (Funk Abwehr, or WNV Funk III) for detection of illegal transmitters. Though not strictly an Abwehr department, and employing various military and police personnel, this service needs to be in constant touch with the Abwehr for obtaining information and passing on its results. (The Sipo and S.D. is interfering now in both these spheres.)

(c)　Offensive Intelligence.

(i)　Mobile Abwehr units operate in the theatre of hostilities in the two offensive sections (this will apply particularly to a retreat in the West):-

I.   Operational intelligence, collected by visual recce, interrogation, telephone interception, seizing documents, using spies and traitors.

II.   Sabotage, guerrilla warfare and subversion, i.e. demoralisation, rumour spreading etc. Personnel of the "Brandenburg Division" are specially trained to carry out such para-military jobs in civilian clothes or in German uniform.

(ii) Static Abwehr H.Q.s employ agents anywhere inside or outside occupied territory to carry out the same duties.

(iii) "R Organisation" prepared for areas from which German forces may have to retreat. Individual agents stay behind to carry out any of the above offensive duties and communicate by W/T with Abwehr posts behind the German lines.

(d)   Importance to the Agent.

Main features and dangers summarised:-

(i)   The main armed forces authority directing measures against subversive activity. Supplies directives and undertakes important investigations.

(ii) Like the S.D. tends to remain more inconspicuous than e.g. the Gestapo, working principally as an information and investigation service.

(iii) Danger of penetration, dating far back, and of longstanding information service.

(iv) Extent of its authority over civilians in C.E. matters generally limited to what is necessary for protecting military targets and conducting investigations. Makes as much use

as possible of G.F.P. Will, however, hand over suspects to
Military Courts Martial and now sometimes to Gestapo.

(v) Liaison therefore to be expected - With military
security police (G.F.P.), its chief instrument in security
work (in Germany the latter work is done by the Gestapo).
With Sipo and S.D. since their work is often closely
connected. Liaison has often been bad owing to jealousy and
difference in outlook.

(vi) Recognition. There is no means of recognition by uniform.
Officers may wear plain clothes where necessary but will
otherwise wear the uniform of the branch of the armed forces
to which they belong. They usually travel with Civil Service
cover. Their papers offer the only material evidence for
identifying them.

2.   GEHEIME FELDPOLIZEI (G.F.P.) - Military Security Police.

(a)   C. E. Work.

(i)   Army or Air Force personnel trained in C.E. Their work is
to protect security of military targets (personnel or material)
against subversive activity, i.e. to see that the C.E. directives
of the Abwehr are carried out. No offensive intelligence work.

(ii) They act as an executive arm responsible to the
intelligence officer at the Army H.Q. to which they are
attached. They may also be attached to a Kommandantur or local
H.Q. of military administration.

(iii) They do investigations into breaches of military
security, preliminary enquiries of their own initiative,
afterwards under higher authority (Abwehr or otherwise).

(iv) They do not carry out routine controls or round-ups but
will supervise the work of the Feldgendarmerie (uniformed

military police) and will receive any reports on suspects from them. Close liaison between the two.

(v)   They are most often ex-members of the German criminal police. Therefore a moderately good standard of intelligence and experience.

(vi) They may carry out investigations into civil C.E. matters, but if so, are most likely to be under the direction of the Sipo and S.D. They may in any case include S.S. men or even Sipo and S.D. personnel.

(vii) Distribution.

Sections (about 35 men) attached to each Army or L of C. H. Q.

Sections (varying strength) in important towns.

Small detached units under Kommandanturs, harbour masters etc.

(b)   Importance to the Agent.

Main features and dangers summarised:-

(i)   Investigation after subversive activity against a military target. Quite capable in this, but initiative in any important matter will come from Abwehr or Sipo and S.D.

(ii) Supervise routine security work of Feldgendarmerie and, where there is military administration, national civil police. Receive reports on suspects from both.

(iii) Powers are quite considerable: - Command where needed over any Army O.R.s.

Access to any military establishment, or means of communication.

Provisional arrest of soldiers or civilians.

(iv) Liaison with:- Feldgendarmerie.

Gestapo (often work under Sipo - S.D. direction).

(v)   Some clandestine work and use of informers, along with routine supervision and investigation work.

(vi) Numbers relatively small, but generally have police experience.

(c)   Recognition.

(i)   Civilian clothes are worn where necessary. In this case identity papers are the only help. Main identity card light blue.

(ii) Where uniform is worn: -

Normal army uniform with colour of arm dark green (as for Wehrmacht official) and secondary colour light blue (on epaulettes). The letters G.F.P. may also be worn on epaulettes.

C. 9(A)

June 1944

INTELLIGENCE REPORTS.

1. GENERAL INSTRUCTIONS.

It is not the essential task of this organisation to collect and transmit military information; but circumstances are likely to arise in which the agent, whether his organisation is paramilitary or otherwise, can render valuable service by doing so. The following limitations must, however, be observed:-

a. He will at no time neglect or prejudice his primary

mission; the information he sends (indicated below) will be obtained in the course of his normal work.

b.   Reports will be simple, non-technical statement of fact, i.e. of what he or others have seen (such as could be based on the outline knowledge contained in the foregoing lectures). He will not attempt to interpret their significance.

c.   Communications before the arrival of Allied forces in his area will be by radio direct to his base in England. It will be by first available "sked" after information is obtained and will receive priority over all routine matters.

d.   Contact with advancing Allied forces will usually be established only when he is picked up by an officer of this organisation. (He will be briefed on this arrangement.) Any information in his possession can then be passed on directly or indirectly to the appropriate military authority.

e.   Unless especially requested, he will confine himself to the subjects undermentioned, and should in any case follow carefully the method indicated.

2.   WHAT TO REPORT.

a.   Concentration.

i.   Concentrations of troops and equipment. (Approximate minimum one regiment i.e. about 3000 men.)

ii.   Position of H.Q.s of regimental level and above. (Note – H.Q. flags: especially division and regiment.)

iii.   Concentrations of aircraft, particularly troop-carriers or gliders.

b.   Movement.

iv.   Large movements of German Air Force flying personnel.

v.   Large movements of troops or equipment (a) by rail, 10 trains upwards (b) by road, convoys of 8 hours upwards.

vi.   Movement of A.F.V.s. more than 50.

vii.   Movement of flotillas of light naval craft and of major naval units.

viii. Important rearrangement of G.A.F. Flak gun positions.

ix.   Establishment of new large dumps – contents and position.

c.   Special measures – military and C.E.

x.   Good evidence of preparations for chemical warfare.

xi.   Information about any important bridges not destroyed by the Germans in withdrawal.

xii. Any details concerning German demolitions, the position of booby-traps, mine-fields, etc. will be extremely valuable to advancing troops.

xiii. Any information regarding agents left behind by the departing Germans.

xiv. Exact location of Gestapo, S.D. Abwehr or G.F.P. H.Qs and their records.

3.   HOW TO REPORT.

a.   Principles.

A report, to be of value, must conform to the following principles:-

i.   Timeliness.

ii.   Get your information through as early as possible.

Conditions change rapidly in war and information will lose its value if delayed.

iii. Do not report things which are likely to be out-of-date by the time they are received; minimum delays of something like 12 hours must be counted upon before a formation in the field could act on a radio message sent by an agent. A brief report at once is always better than a detailed report too late.

iv. Clarity.

Extreme care in wording to avoid possibility of confusion.

v. Brevity.

The report should be as short as is consistent with clarity. Use telegraphic wording but avoid any doubt as to meaning.

vi. Accuracy.

It goes without saying that an agent must never invent, never exaggerate, never quote as facts things for which there is only hear-say evidence. But above all he must beware of these failings in others: vanity invariably tends to produce them, especially in civilians offering military information.

When reporting second-hand evidence always mention that information is second-hand and state quality of source.

vii. Detail.

Vague and general information is of no value whatever. The words "some", "many", "a few", "a lot", etc. have no place in a good report.

Quote facts and figures even if approximate. Qualify all estimates or assumptions.

Where it is not possible to identify, use should be made of descriptions, never of guess-work.

The above qualities apply as much to written reports as to wireless messages. If ever the former are used, the value of sketches and sketch-maps cannot be overestimated.

b. Formula for Reporting.

If the following formula is adopted when recording what you have observed, or when obtaining information from another source, the important points will be covered (although certain additional detail may be required in individual cases). Ask yourself, or your informant, these questions:-

Q. Where?

A. Exact location of object or events (map reference where possible).

Q. When?

A. Time and date of events observed.

Q. Who or what?

A. Identity or description of object of observation.

Q. How many or how much?

A. Estimated number or quantity, i.e. numerically in case of troops, not in terms of formations. Approximate limits can at least be given, e.g. "between 5000 and 10,000".

As stated above, avoid attempting to answer the question: "Why?": deductions are dangerous and useless unless based on information which is certain, and an authority fully qualified to judge.

Finally read through your report, putting yourself in the position of the recipient, and decide whether, if you knew nothing of the circumstances, you would understand the message perfectly without any shadow of doubt.

c. Example of Bad Report. (Arrival of troops in small town of X).

"Thursday. A lot of German troops arrived here recently and appear to be resting. Some of them have artillery. Otherwise there seems to be nothing unusual about them. It would seem they were likely to withdraw further eastwards. I heard their commander had been killed and that their morale is not so good".

Value of report: Nil.

d. Example of Good Report. (Same events observed in X.)

"17.10.44. At 2200 16.10.44 I saw following German Army units arrive in X by main road from west. Normal infantry uniform. No. 337 and No. 724 on shoulder. Estimated number 5,000 to 7,000 horse-drawn transport. Twelve 75 mm. infantry howitzers seen. Vehicles marked with following signs and numbers ... Troops appeared very tired. Billeted North-West quarter of X. Excellent source states they are resting after service in front line at Y."

Students can finally write a specimen brief report on information given.

C. 9(B)

June 1944

SABOTAGE OF ENEMY ROAD SIGNS

(The following explanatory remarks will suffice to precede a study of sabotage Handbook Vol. 7.)

This is another para-military operation which requires little technical skill and which almost any organiser and any section of the civil population are capable of undertaking.

1. AIM.

To cause confusion amongst enemy road transport, i.e.

bottlenecks and hold-ups which can have serious effect at a vital moment. It may be combined with actual sabotage and destruction of enemy vehicles, but this is a much more complicated operation.

2. REQUIREMENTS FOR MAXIMUM RESULT.

a. Co-ordinated action over a vital area, to avoid undue movement by individuals.

b. Correct timing, when enemy transport movement is at its height. i.e. especially hours of darkness which are also safest.

c. Simple methods, involving no particular intelligence, little or no instruction and no undue risk; even women and children should be able to assist.

d. Removal of signs, rather than alteration or substitution, is thus recommended.

3. AREAS INVOLVED.

a. Forward areas - unfavourable because of difficulty of movement, and large concentrations of troops.

b. Base areas - also offer little scope because of intense police activity, and because M.T. drivers get to know the area well.

c. Lines of communication. - by far the best possibilities, because they cover a large area, difficult to police, troops less concentrated and drivers not so familiar with the area.

4. TYPES OF SIGN, each of which suggest different methods (show detailed, examples in handbook).

a. Diversion signs.

e.g. Make columns converge or meet, or combine with sabotage.

b. Warning signs.

e.g. cause halts and delay by warnings of mines, booby traps,
guerrillas; or destruction by removing warnings; cause delay
or accident by altering carrying-capacity of bridges.

c. Danger signs.

e.g. cause accidents by alteration or removal, or combine with
sabotage.

d. Direction signs.

e.g. removal, substitution, or alteration of signs to
delivery, filling, repair and parking places etc.

e. Speed limit signs.

e.g. cause delay or accident by indicating presence or absence
of certain obstacles or dangers.

f. Unit and formation signs and flags.

Individual must really know his area to make it worth while
tampering with these, and must do it sparingly.

Such well timed and co-ordinated action would obviously
produce best results, but even random widespread removal of
signs would make worth-while confusion.

C.12

July 44

RECOGNITION OF ENEMY FORCES' UNIFORMS.

REVISION.

Students practise the identification from photographs of
all German uniforms mentioned in Police, Party, and Armed

Forces lectures, this is a useful conclusion to the course, summarising the main features required for the recognition of all the above types of personnel; - essential knowledge for the agent's self-protection, and for the obtaining of useful information.

A comprehensive collection of photographs is grouped as follows:-

1. Police.
    (a) German Uniformed Police.
    (b) German C.E. authorities in uniform.
    (c) National police of occupied countries.

2. Nazi Party
    (a) German organisations.
    (b) Organisations of occupied countries.
    (c) Waffen S.S. - German and foreign.

3. Armed Forces.
    (a) German Army.
    (b) German air force.
    (c) Foreign volunteers.

D. 1
July 1944

MORALE WARFARE.

A. INTRODUCTORY.

Object of lectures.

- To explain the possibilities of this form of attack on the enemy.

- To describe the methods, especially those which can be used by the agent.

- To indicate the campaigns with which the agent is most concerned.

The agent may be instructed to co-operate in organising some of the activities covered in these lectures.

B. MORALE WARFARE.

Has dual aim:

i. maintaining morale (of Allies and friends).

ii. destroying morale (of enemies).

Close relation which has always existed between morale warfare and physical warfare, i.e:

i. They are complementary. One attacks the will, the other the means, to fight.

ii. New weapons and new tactics often have more value psychologically than physically, e.g. tanks, dive-bombers, guerrilla warfare.

iii. Morale warfare prepares and exploits military victory.

C. MORALE.

Since the aim is to influence morale, the importance and basis of morale must be examined.

i. Morale is important because, even in modern war, the human element is paramount. Will to work and will to fight necessary to make and man the machines. If the enemy's will to work and fight is broken the war is won.

ii. Morale is founded on a belief in:

a. The power – arms, victories, allies, comrades etc.

106

b. The competence – officers, political leaders, administrators, workers etc.

c. The value or worth-whileness – cause, methods employed, esprit de corps etc.

In order, therefore, to attack enemy morale or to stimulate the morale of our friends we must bear these factors in mind and see how they are related to the individual group we wish to affect.

D. PROPAGANDA.

A powerful weapon of morale warfare used to further policy even before physical warfare begins.

> Example: German power diplomacy and propaganda in 1938 leading to:

> > annexation of Austria and Czechoslovakia.

> In war propaganda to foreign countries is an integral part of strategy. It consists of:

1. Open methods – Radio, and leaflets dropped by aircraft.

2. Clandestine methods – clandestine literature, rumour etc.

> The latter, undertaken by the agent, is an essential part of propaganda. Close relation of two types of method.

Example from past: German 1940 campaign. Open propaganda giving facts and emphasising invincible might of German arms.

Clandestine propaganda stimulating division of allies, despondency and panic.

Example for future: Western Front. Open propaganda describes hopelessness of German position.

Clandestine propaganda spreads rumours of German disaster, distributes "sauf-conduits" to soldiers.

Clandestine methods will be discussed in detail in the next lecture.

E. TECHNIQUES OF PROPAGANDA.

There are two techniques of approach in propaganda:

1. White Propaganda which emanates from an authentic source, e.g. from an Allied Government, a resistance movement, etc. This will be founded on truth.

Examples:

R.A.F. leaflets.

B.B.C. broadcasts.

Clandestine Press.

2. Black Propaganda which emanates from an ostensibly enemy source, through in fact it is produced by us. This will not necessarily be founded on truth but will always be plausible.

Examples:

Radio station which purports to transmit from enemy territory.

Forged leaflets, apparently printed by illegal Axis movements, providing instructions on how to malinger, desert or mutiny.

Forged military or administrative orders.

Rumours or slogans which appear to originate from the enemy.

Black propaganda is only used against the enemy.

1. Subversion of enemy forces.

2. Trojan Horse - Foreign workers campaign.

3. Passive resistance in Occupied counteries.

4. Tasks preparatory to Allied arrival.

G. CONCLUSION.

These lectures will explain the various campaigns so that the agent may encourage them where possible and, if able to assist them himself, may understand how his role fits in with the plan.

D.2/3
January 1944

METHODS OF MORALE WARFARE.

A. INTRODUCTION.

This lecture will deal with the individual methods of Morale Warfare, irrespective of whether they are used to destroy enemy morale or raise the morale of the occupied countries, under the following headings:

1. Exterior Propaganda.

2. Interior or Clandestine Propaganda.

B. EXTERIOR PROPAGANDA.

Since this does not directly concern the agent in the field, it will only be discussed briefly. Main methods are:

1. Radio. Disseminates all types of mass propaganda both to occupied countries and to the enemy. Influence due largely to its reputation for truth and authority. Patriots must be encouraged to obey it and to make provision against confiscation of sets. Note: Radio can be "black" or "white".

2. R.A.F. Leaflet. Disseminates all types of mass propaganda both to occupied countries and to the enemy. Has a more regional effect than the B.B.C. Influence due largely to reputation of R.A.F. Patriots must be encouraged to pass on R.A.F. literature to sympathisers. Certain types to be posted to German troops or administrators.

C. INTERIOR OR CLANDESTINE PROPAGANDA.

Either printed in the field (refer to recruiting printers and use of clandestine printing sets) or sent by container. Necessity for obtaining supplies of paper and type. Main methods are:

1. Clandestine Newspapers.

Principal value to raise and control morale; instructional propaganda; listing collaborators and agents provocateurs. (Examples to be shown.)

Method of distribution: posting in trade "circular" envelopes.

2. Tracts.

Can be either "black" or "white".

a. "White" Tracts. Principally used to appeal to specific group of population to take defined action providing publicity of allied war effort or resistance movement to enemy or friendly groups. When tract is intended as an appeal, a method of writing is:

Title: Appeal to group, stating importance of subject.

Grievances: Principal local grievance or grievances which have occasioned the appeal.

Hope: Worthwhileness or value of action or lack of action.

Action: The orders to be conveyed.

Signature: Authoritative source.

Methods of distribution: Dependent on circumstances; organised distribution service; jetsam method (i.e. phone boxes, lavatories, cafes etc.); postal distribution in packets to known sympathisers; scattered distribution at night in defined district or in high wind.

b. "Black" Tracts. Value largely due to their subversive nature – inciting the enemy to take subversive action, which he believes to come from his own compatriots, or spreading disunity; usually forgeries of military or administrative orders or invented illegal organisation among the enemy troops.

Methods of distribution: More limited number required – one or two left officially or in error in places which are frequented by the enemy. In addition to methods as for "white" tracts, these can be posted on notice-boards, walls etc.; left slightly charred and crumpled on office floors or in waiting-rooms; left among other literature in hotels etc.; left, as if in error or negligence, in packets in cafes, waiting-rooms, taxis, trains etc. (e.g. packet of official tracts marked "For Officers Only").

3. Anonymous Letters.

Used against individual enemies, either German troops or collaborators; objects: threats and denunciations combined with model coffins, anonymous phone calls etc.; disguised handwriting; threatening tone and source. Example: Belgian burgomaster. Technique of approach: "black" or "white".

Method of distribution: by post (for security precautions, see "A" lectures).

4. Chain Letter.

Used to circularise a specific group – e.g. German troops or patriots; objects: passing instructions on desertion, warnings of a general nature (superstition or prophecies), items of censored news (largely used in Norway and Holland where radios have been confiscated); disguised handwriting; short and legible; containing security instructions and copying instructions. Technique of approach: "black" or "white".

Method of distribution: by post (security precautions).

5. Slogans.

Chalked on walls; written on shop windows (camouflaged frosting material) etc.; used (i.e. German illegal source); chalk pictures and rhymes can also be used. Used in conjunction with other forms of clandestine propaganda.

Method of use: dusk or dawn, by youths acting under instructions.

6. Stickers.

Printed in this country and sent by container. Used for stimulation of morale, short instructions, threats, ridicule or "black" use – combined with other forms of clandestine propaganda.

Method of use: dusk or dawn, on notice-boards, walls, windows or lamp-posts.

7.   Stencils.

Cut out of cardboard or linoleum. Can be used for raising
morale, causing confusion or defacing German or collaborators'
instructions.

Method of use: dusk or dawn.

8.   Rumours.

German abuse of truth in news services has resulted in
considerable success of rumour tactics. Rumours provide
the clandestine propaganda services with invaluable arm for
demoralisation, but they should be used carefully and under
directive only. Rumours containing specific promises of
allied action or post-war planning will never be spread unless
authoritatively directed.

General Principles.

a.   Constructions.

i.   Satisfaction of current mood. A good rumour will appeal
to the current desires and feelings – the type of thing people
want to hear. It must be timed to fit into the mood. It is
useless to spread a defeatist rumour after a German victory or
reassuring speech.

ii.   Appeal to feelings rather than intellect. Emotional
longings (end of war, leave); confirm suspicions (party
orgies, might of allied arms); superstitious instincts
(prophecies); pornographic instincts (relations of F.W.'s
and German women); fears and grievances (bombing, Russian
front).

iii. Basis of truth. Mixture of truth and fiction lends
plausibility. (E.g. "The news of the R. A. F. bombings has
been played down so as not to lower morale" (true) "because

the new explosive they are using is causing widespread nervous breakdowns; the lunatic-asylums are full" (fictions).)

iv.   Must not be too long. Easily repeatable and not liable to over-exaggeration. Danger of figures.

v.   Authoritative source. Appears to bear the hall-mark of authenticity. (E.g. "a police agent told a man I met ...")

vi.   Must be dramatic – worthy of repetition. (E.g. "A ward-maid from the Stettin lunatic asylum, who has just come home, says that the inventor of Pervitin shot himself when he discovered that all who take it go slowly mad or become impotent.")

b.   Placing a Rumour. The rumour must be placed in the direction of the group who are intended to hear it.

The rumour should be whispered only once by the original "rumour-monger".

The "rumour-monger" should choose "fertile" ground for his rumour (e.g. hair-dresser, dentist, bar-maid, prostitute, queue outside a shop etc.).

The source of the rumour should be placed as far away as possible to prevent verification or "checking up". (E.g. "A man I met in the bus told me ...")

Care must be taken to introduce the rumour naturally in conversation. Wherever possible arrange for the interception of the rumour later to observe its effect.

A series of "rumour-mongers" can be employed to whisper the rumour, each applying the above rules.

9.   Fortune-Telling.

Used against enemy troops, particularly U-boat crews, pilots

etc. Genuine fortune tellers to be recruited; or handing on
horoscopes, saying they have been sold to you.

10. Sympathetic Conversations.

Certain specified subjects (e.g. bombing of Germany, Russian
front etc.) to be discussed with enemy troops by persons who
can safely contact them, to spread demoralisation; must give
impression of being genuinely pro-German and conversation must
not be satirical or sarcastic. Intelligent agents required.
"Loose" talk on the part of the soldier should be discouraged.

11. "Isolation" Tactics.

Encouragement of population to isolate and ridicule German
troops; encouragement can be achieved by "whispering" campaign
or carefully setting an example (e.g. Dutch "watch" trick);
threats to women who consort with German troops; use of
"stink" bombs, itching powder.

. CONCLUSION.

These methods will be discussed in relation to targets during
the later lectures. It is important to realise that they must
be used as parts of a campaign and not as individual forms of
attack. It is the combination of pinpricking tactics used on a
mass scale which produces an effective result.

D. 7
July 1944

PASSIVE RESISTANCE IN OCCUPIED COUNTRIES.

. INTRODUCTION.

Allied propaganda encourages passive resistance on the part of all those not already organised in active groups.

Large-scale passive resistance is very effective:

i.   Materially (i.e. causing drop in production, delay, etc.).

ii.   Psychologically (i.e. encourages patriots, exasperates occupying power).

B. OPPORTUNITIES.

Three principal spheres of opportunity, in following order of importance:

i.   Transport, communication and vital installations.

ii.   Industry.

iii.   Administration.

C. PRESENT SITUATION.

i.   Transport and Communications.

Roads, railways, telephones, telegraph and power systems indispensable to German military operations.

All above are vulnerable to Passive Resistance as well as to active sabotage.

Evidence that damage to installations by air bombardment and by sabotage has already affected operations in the West.

ii.   Industry.

Germany's position difficult owing to:

German manpower problem,

Allied bombing of German industry.

Sabotage usually the most effective means of denying Germany the fruits of industrial output, but not always the best means:

a). Where dangers exceed probable results,

b). Where reprisals and deportations are to be avoided.

In these cases passive resistance can be undertaken and will be effective.

Note: - Anti-transport campaign also prevents a large proportion of local production from reaching Germany.

iii. Administration.

Germany cannot administer occupied territories without the collaborators in Government and Civil Service. She depends on the support of all grades of civil service, police, judiciary etc.

Passive Resistance in this sphere (already taken to some extent on specific measures, e.g. in France on the Relève) will:

a). Allow resistance movements to operate in greater safety.

b). Irritate and frustrate German functionaries.

METHODS.

i. By employees in above spheres:

GO-SLOW TACTICS.

Best method of organising Go-Slow is by contacting old Trades Union leaders. Concentration on bottle-necks in industry (which varies according to the sphere).

Examples:

a). Transport and Communications

- especially in loading and unloading trains and vehicles,

- transposing labels,

- altering date of last lubrication on railway wagons,

- removing notices as "Breakable", "This side up with care" etc.,

- mistakes in sorting mail.

b). Industry.

Personnel factory offices can add to these activities by

- apparent stupidity and inefficiency,

- prolonging correspondence,

- forgetfulness.

c). Administration.

- unnecessary "red-tape"

- loss of documents

- concentration on irrelevant criminal activities

- procrastination.

Note. Discuss simple examples.

Note. Possible to maintain constant high level of passive resistance. According to turn of events it should be increase or modified. Strikes with limited objectives feasible in certain circumstances e.g. Copenhagen strikes, Italian strikes.

ii. By all sections of the population, to assist above campaigns.

a). Anonymous Letters.

i. To collaborators - congratulations for resistance work (letter not marked "Private") - threats of assassination or sabotage.

ii. To police - denouncing Quislings for underground activities - reporting plots and imaginary incidents.

b). Slogans, stickers, stencils.

i. Ridicule and threats to collaborators - "Ici habite un collaborateur".

ii. Administrative sabotage - "Cancelled" on official notices.

c). Rumours.

For demoralisation of collaborators, e.g. "Milice is not trusted by Germany and will be sent to Eastern front".

d). Anonymous telephone calls.

e.g. - cancelling orders,

- threatening or reporting sabotage at given time or place.

e). Numbers of "genuine" but unnecessary enquiries at prefectures etc. by post, telephone or in person.

f). Clandestine press and tracts (where suitable) sent to collaborators. E.g. black lists, allied statements etc.

E. PASSIVE RESISTANCE DURING PERIODS OF CONFUSION.

After or during an air-raid or in the period immediately prior to liberation false reports on the following lines can be used (cf. German 1940 Campaign):

i. Lights seen at night.

ii. Parachutists seen descending.

iii. Guerrilla activities.

iv. Unexploded bombs.

v. German personnel buried under debris.

These would be personal reports to minor officials, junior officers, N.C.O.s etc. made by innocent-looking persons who appeared frightened.

F. CONCLUSION.

Above activities are complementary to work of active resistance. Agents should direct and encourage them where possible. Many patriots not prepared to join active groups able and willing to undertake this form of resistance.

CODES AND CIPHERS.

The object is to provide each agent with code and cipher systems suited to his requirements and capabilities and at the same time to maintain the maximum cryptographic security.

The student is first taught the basic systems and the instructor then decides which operational variations are most suited to him. The systems chosen vary according to the ability and memory of the student, the language to be used, the type of work, and the country in which the student is going to operate.

It is therefore essential to have available a wide selection of systems and to add to them as often as possible. The simultaneous use of a number of different systems also has the advantage of making the enemy cryptographer's task more difficult.

With this system, each student is given a personal identity prefix and a security check, so that the origin of the message can be established and its authenticity guaranteed.

CODES, CIPHERS, SECRET INK AND CENSORSHIP.

INTRODUCTION.

Communications form a vital part of any organisation, and you will consider the whole question of communications in one of the lectures upon organisation.

This, and the following lectures, will be concerned with the more technical point of view - particular code and cipher systems, secret inks and methods of censorship.

GENERAL PRINCIPLES.

(a) The need for Security.

It is essential to reduce to a minimum evidence that codes, ciphers or secret inks are being used. Never keep papers used to encipher or decipher messages or notes of the details of the systems used.

Do not keep prepared solutions of secret inks. Make them up from the innocent materials as they are required.

Always use the prearranged security check in messages and be certain that it is correct. Remember it is the only proof to the receiver that the message is genuine.

If communicating with more than one person have separate arrangements for each.

Never disclose any personal arrangements for communicating by codes or ciphers.

(b) The Need for Care.

Great care is needed in using codes and ciphers. One error may result in the message being indecipherable and cause a serious loss of time.

Always check your work by deciphering the completed message before you send it.

(c) The Need for Concealment.

In certain cases it is necessary to carry printed material for cipher systems. To aid concealment this is specially camouflaged, but every additional precaution should be taken to avoid its discovery.

DEFINITIONS.

For the purposes of our work, codes and ciphers may be distinguished as follows:-

A cipher is a method of converting a message into symbols which do not appear innocent, and which have no meaning to a person not possessing the key.

A code is a method of concealing a message in such a way as to make it appear innocent. It is a cipher hidden in an apparently innocent communication, such as a letter.

SYSTEMS.

According to individual requirements a number of the following systems will be explained:-

a). Simple Word Code.

b). Playfair Cipher.

c). Multi-Alphabet Cipher.

d). Switch Cipher.

e). Innocent Letter Code.

f). Double Transposition Cipher.

g). Variations on the Double Transposition Cipher.

1. W.O.K. system.

2. Mental W.O.K. Systems I, II, IV and V.

3. Mental Indicator Systems.

4. Code 53.

h). Letter One-Time Pad Cipher.

i). Mental Pad System.

j). Vocabulary Systems.

For all operational conventions on the above systems the necessary individual security checks and identity arrangements will be made.

SIMPLE WORD CODE

A simple word code is the arrangement by conventions of certain words or phrases to mean other words or phrases. Only a limited variety of messages can be sent by such a code as this.

When used:-

a). Telegraph.

b). Telephone.

c). Personal advertisement.

d). Post card or letter.

Examples:-

A.   In a post card or letter.

The introduction of an agreed name, word or phrase into the text of the letter will give the pre-arranged message.

e.g. The name "John" might mean - "I am going into hiding immediately."

B.   In a telegram.

NO NEWS RECEIVED FOR AGES ARE YOU WELL

might be agreed to mean

CARRY ON WITH THE SCHEME AS ARRANGED.

C.   On the telephone.

Veiled language would usually be sufficient, but code names can also be used; e.g. two hours might be added to the time of any rendezvous.

D.   In a Personal Advertisement.

"Bicycle for sale, apply 6 Rue de la Croix" might be a general warning to all members not to visit the organiser until further notice.

Note: It would, in such cases, be necessary to be able to produce a bicycle if required. A "lost" advertisement is very suitable, as it produces no reply.

PLAYFAIR CIPHER.

a).   Characteristics.

(a)   Easily memorisable.

(b)   Easy to operate.

(c)   Secure for short messages.

b).   Uses.

i).   For concealment in an innocent communication, such as a
letter, in internal or external correspondence. This is its
principal use. Conventions will be arranged with you, which
you may use for the purpose of communication from the field to
this country.

ii). For sending a message through the W/T Operator to this
country, which the operator will not understand, e.g. address
of organiser. This will be re-enciphered by the operator.
This procedure is complicated and should not be used except to
serve a real need.

Note. The system is not sufficiently secure to use as a
straight cipher unless the message is extremely short - less
than 70 letters.

c).   Method - attached.

This cipher, first used during the 1914-18 war, combines high
security with comparative simplicity. It is based on a square
grille, containing 25 cells.

KEYWORDS.

The keyword may be a word or phrase and should contain not
less than 8 different letters and include two of the last
6 letters of the alphabet. The keyword is written into the
square. Any letters which recur are omitted.

Example:

KEYWORD: SUPPLEMENTARY.

```
------------
   SUPLE
------------
   MNTAR
------------
     Y
------------
------------
------------
```

The remaining letters of the alphabet are then written in to
complete the cage. As we have only 25 squares, one letter has
to be suppressed.

```
------------
   SUPLE
------------
   MNTAR
------------
   YBCDF
------------
   GHIJK
------------
   OQVWX
------------
```

TO ENCIPHER.

Divide the message to be enciphered into groups of two
letters, e.g.:

ARRIVE CHARING CROSS AT FIVE

AR RI VE CH AR IN GC RO SS AT FI VE

126

When the same letter occurs twice in a group (as above –
"SS"), the two letters must be separated by a null or dud
letter which has previously been selected for this purpose.
When one letter is left over at the end of the message, the
group is made up by adding a further dud letter. Example:

AR RI VE CH AR IN GC RO SX SA TF IV EX

There are three possible ways in which a pair of letters may
occur in the square – on the same horizontal line; in the same
vertical column; as opposite corners of a rectangle.

1. Letters on the same horizontal line. Substitute the letter
immediately on the right. Example:

NA – TR

HI – IJ

JG – KH

When the last letter of a line is to be changed, return to the
beginning of the same line. Examples:

MR – NM

QX – VO

2. Letters in the same vertical column. Substitute the letter
immediately below. Examples:-

LD – AJ

BH – HQ

When the bottom letter of a column is to be changed, return to the head of the column. Examples:

NQ – BU

EX – RE

3. Pairs of letters forming opposite corners of a rectangle. Take the two letters which form the other two corners of the rectangle, starting on the same level as the first letter of the pair in the clear text. Examples:

```
              ------------
   YJ – DG    SUPLE
              ------------
   AF – RD    MNTAR
              ------------
   XL – WE    YBCDF
              ------------
   RS – ME    GHIJK
              ------------
              OQVWX
              ------------
```

COMPLETED EXAMPLE.

AR RI VE CH AR IN GC RO SX SA TF IV EX

RM TK XP BI RM HT IY MX EO LM RC VP RE

TO DECIPHER.

1. Take the keyword and complete the square, omitting the agreed letter.

2. Divide the cipher message into pairs.

3. Substitute the pairs into the square, performing the reverse movements to encipherment - i.e:

a. Horizontal line - move to LEFT.

b. Vertical line - move UP.

c. Opposite Corners of Rectangle. Follow the same procedure exactly as for enciphering.

NUMBERS.

1. If the number to be sent is short, for example, "SEND FIVE CONTAINERS," it is best to spell it out as in this message.

2. If, however, the number is long, for example, "MAP REF. 873481" it is preferable to replace the figures by letters on an agreed table. A simple table would be:

A	B	C	D	E	F	G	H	I	J
1	2	3	4	5	6	7	8	9	10

It is necessary to preface these letters by an indicator group to show that the letters represent figures, e.g. NR, NO, FIG. It is also necessary to insert a similar, but different, group at the end of the letters representing the figures. For example:

"MY ADDRESS IS 297 RUE DE LA PAIX"

"MY ADDRESS IS NRBIGNO RUE DE LA PAIX"

The message is then divided into pairs and enciphered as usual.

SECRET INKS.

1. DEFINITIONS.

High-Grade Inks.

These are inks made of rare or complicated chemicals, unobtainable in the field. When used they must be taken from this country in some concealed form, such as a button or toothpaste.

When necessary, particular instruction is given in the use of these inks.

Simple Inks.

These are inks which can be made from materials obtainable in the field under innocent cover.

A number will be taught and demonstrated.

2. PURPOSE.

Secret Inks are useful in two ways:-

a) By post, in external communication only.

To send through the post, via a neutral country, a message which would be too long to send by innocent letter code; or which contains maps or drawings.

For this purpose a high-grade ink must be used.

In internal post, no inks should normally be used.

The reason for this distinction is that -

i. in external mail it is not necessary to give the enemy any means of tracing the letter to any part of the organisation, other than the neutral address, whereas

ii. in internal mail the receiving end of the line is inevitably compromised if the ink is suspected.

b) By courier.

To conceal a message carried by a courier, either from one country to another or within a country. If a compromising message, or a cipher, must be carried in writing, it is safer for the courier if it is written in secret ink. High-grade or simple inks may be used for this purpose.

WRITING MATERIAL.

a) Choice of paper. In general, as good a quality of note-paper as possible should be used. The following types should be avoided:-

i. Paper with very shiny surface.

ii. Absorbent paper.

b) Choice of nibs. The ideal nib is ball-pointed, but this should not be used as it is an incriminating article. An ordinary nib of the Waverley type is adequate.

The nib should preferably be of stainless steel and must be perfectly clean when used.

A sharpened match-stick may also be used.

TECHNIQUE OF WRITING.

a) The paper should be placed on a hard, smooth surface, e.g. glass or a mahogany table.

b) The writer should work with the writing between eye and light so that the characters can be seen as they are written.

c) Cover up that part of the paper on which the hand is

resting. Avoid pressing. It should be impossible to hear the pen as it moves across the paper.

d) There is only one standard that is satisfactory - absolute invisibility.

5. WHERE TO WRITE SECRET MESSAGE.

This will vary greatly with the circumstances. The following examples are given:-

a) Under the cover of an ordinary letter. This is the obvious and best way for messages passing through the post. In this case the secret message may occupy many different positions on the letter, such as:-

i. Across the lines of the covering letter; between the lines is very inadvisable. (Covering letter is, of course, written afterwards.)

ii. On the back.

iii.On the inside of the envelope.

b) On a newspaper.

c) Within a split postcard.

d) For a courier, on an old letter or document.

6. Here follow details of inks taught.

7. CENSORSHIP TESTS.

(This may be omitted if time is insufficient, and if high-grade inks are not to be used. It is essential if high-grade inks have been taught.)

The main routine tests of the censorship are:-

a) Preliminary Examination. Usually carried out by women, who look for anything suspicious in the way of strange wording, scratches on the paper, etc. Observance of the principles already taught will be adequate protection against this test.

b) Examination under ultra-violet light. Some inks are invisible to the naked eye under ordinary light but fluoresce and are clearly visible under ultra-violet light. None of the inks taught (except wax) behave thus, but almost all inks are liable to be detected under ultra-violet light if they are used in an excessively strong solution.

To protect a message against this test, therefore, it is necessary to reduce the strength of the ink to the minimum mixture compatible with legibility.

c) Iodine Developer. This test is by far the most dangerous. The developer will reveal any disturbances of the fibres of the surface of the paper, and such disturbances will be created both by passing a dry pen over the paper and by the dropping of plain water on to the paper (this can be demonstrated).

3. PROTECTION AGAINST GENSORSHIP TESTS.

To mask the disturbance created by the pen and ink, disturb all the fibres of the paper in the following manner:-

a). Rub the paper on both sides with particular attention to the actual spot in which is the secret writing. If this procedure is followed it will be better not to use ruled paper, as the lines may disappear with rubbing.

b). Either (i) steam the paper (this is the better method) or (ii) damp the paper with wet cotton wool.

c). Press the paper between two sheets of blotting paper under a weight.

It may not always be necessary to carry out all these protective measures, for example in the case of messages carried by a courier who is not likely to pass any control post. But it is always safer to do so.

9. SUMMARY OF METHOD.

The following are the steps necessary to send a message in secret ink when the full protective measures are followed:-

a). Write two copies of the secret message.

b). Rub and steam or damp both copies.

c). Dry and press both copies.

d). Develop one copy with the specific developer of the ink.

e). If satisfactory, i.e. if neither too weak nor too strong, write the covering letter, and send.

SIMPLE SECRET INKS

1. LEAD ACETATE.

(a) The Ink.

Sugar of lead or lead acetate can be used diluted to a solution of .25 per cent. It should never be used above .5 per cent.

Cover. It can sometimes be obtained as Goulard's lotion for sprains and bruises. It is also used in the painting trade for removing paint.

(b)   The Developer.

It is developed by contact with hydrogen sulphide gas which is given off by any soluble sulphide, e.g. ammonium sulphide. 10 per cent. In water is good solution.

Cover. Sulphides may be obtained in two innocent forms:-

(i)   A depilatory, for example Veet or some similar preparation; squeeze a little of the paste on to a saucer and add two or three drops of white vinegar. Mix the paste with the liquid and lightly swab the paper on which there is invisible writing.

(ii) In horticulture a solution of polysulphides is used for spraying fruit trees.

INK H.

A careful choice of paper is required, one with a glossy surface being preferable.

The letters of the enciphered message which is to be hidden are concealed in pencil beneath the ink of a normal piece of correspondence. The easiest method to adopt is first to write a note in rough and then underline the letters which are to be part of the message. Rewrite, in thick ink writing, inserting in the appropriate positions the letters in pencil. These are afterwards covered in ink. When the whole is dry, rub away any pencil marks which remain. The whole note should be carefully examined to see that no break or thickened lines make any of the letters conspicuous.

To Develop.

Bathe the sheet of paper in any strong bleaching solution (sodium hyperchlorite, parazone, eau de javelle). After some

time (up to two minutes) the ink will be bleached away and
letters in pencil alone remain.

3. ALUM.

The ink should be used at a 1 per cent. solution. It is
developed by heat.

Cover. Can be obtained in the form of a styptic pencil for use
after shaving.

4. PHENOLPHTHALEIN.

(a)   The Ink.

One grain (1/15 of a gram) of phenolphthalein should be
dissolved in a mixture of 10 ccs. of ammonia and 30 ccs. of
water. That is to say, a solution of 1/5th per cent. In one
part ammonia and three parts water.

Cover.

(i)   Phenolphthalein is an aperient and is usually sold in
tablet form, each tablet in this country containing 2 grains
or 2/15ths of a gram.

(ii) Ammonia can be bought for domestic cleaning.

(b)   Developer.

It is developed by a saturated solution of washing soda.

Cover. For domestic use.

5. WAXPAPER.

(a)   Cover. Used for wrapping food products, chocolate,
tobacco, etc. If unobtainable, it can be made by lightly

smearing Vaseline, or even candle grease, on to an ordinary piece of paper.

(b) Developer.

Powdered carbon or graphite (ordinary soot will do).

Cover. Vegetable carbon for medicinal purposes; scrapings from a piece of burnt wood; pencil lead scrapings.

8.12.43

LETTER-OPENING.

NTRODUCTION.

Most censorship is open – that is, the envelope will be cut open, the identity of the censor unit will be shown, either by pencil figures or a stamp, and a label will be used to reseal the envelope. In some cases there may be evidence of testing for writing in secret ink.

This censorship is applied to nearly all external mail. In the case of internal mail, mobile units are employed and they cover different areas for short periods only. They are often used in an area for two or three weeks following disturbances or acts of sabotage or during military exercises or movements.

USE OF SECRET CENSORSHIP.

Secret censorship is applied only to correspondence of people who have been "black-listed". They may be suspected of black-market activities, communism or other political activities, or of being concerned with underground organisations.

A knowledge of the methods employed may be useful to you from two points of view:

a. Defensively. If you realise your mail is being opened in this way it is a warning that you are under suspicion.

b. Offensively. You may be in a position to obtain information from official or other correspondence.

The method may be considered under five headings:

1. Opening the envelope.

2. Resealing the envelope.

3. Recognising interference.

4. Defensive measures.

5. Seals.

1. Opening the Envelope.

Materials necessary:

Clean blotting-paper.

Stainless steel knitting-needle. (A wooden pen-holder which has been thinned down will serve.)

Kettle of boiling water.

Method:

a. If possible open the envelope without using steam; you are less likely to leave traces, particularly in the case of thin or highly-glazed envelopes. Keep the envelope flat, insert the knitting-needle under the flap and roll it gently round the edge. Do not attempt to force the flap and avoid lifting it. Force used on the flap will tear the surface of the envelope and this is impossible to conceal. Make sure your hands are clean.

b. If it is necessary to use steam, do so in small quantities at a time. Localise the steaming as much as possible and avoid

the lower half of the envelope, as the machine-gummed edge of
the lower flap is easily affected. A jacket of blotting-paper
will minimise this risk.

2. Resealing the Envelope.

Materials necessary:

New envelopes or spirit gum.

Clean blotting-paper.

Hot iron.

A flat weight.

Method:

a. If possible reseal with the original gum.

b. If necessary add new gum to the flap either by moistening
the gum on a new envelope and rubbing this along the flap or
by adding ordinary spirit gum with a piece of paper. Care
should be taken not to leave traces of the additional gum on
the surface of the envelope and not to over-run the clearly-
defined edge of the original gummed area.

c. Replace the flap carefully, making sure there are no traces
of gum round the edge of the flap. Do not press on the damp
flap; turn the envelope over and press on the address side.
Place the envelope on a flat surface under a weight for a few
minutes to flatten it out again.

d. If the steam has cockled or dulled the envelope, put
it between two sheets of blotting-paper and press with a
moderately hot iron.

3. Recognising Interference.

It is not easy to detect whether your correspondence has been opened, but an accumulation of small signs may give cause for suspicion. The following are possible indications:

a.   Delay in the Post. If your correspondence begins to arrive by a later delivery than normally, it is possible the delay is due to secret censorship. This is a more definite indication in the case of internal mail than in foreign correspondence.

b.   Use of an Agreed Sign. Avoid obvious tricks such as the insertion of ash or hair in the letter. These will be noticed by the censor and will merely confirm his suspicions.

Some special method of sealing the enveloped might be used, such as leaving a small portion of the gummed surface unsealed. If opened and resealed the special sign would be destroyed by steaming.

c.   Examination of Envelope. By using the same type of envelope regularly correspondents are more likely to notice any irregularities due to clandestine opening.

i.   General appearance. When steam has been used it is possible that the surface of the envelope will be dulled or cockled. This is particularly so in the case of glazed or very thin envelopes.

ii.   The upper flap. This flap is the most likely place to find traces of opening. The edge of the flap may show slight traces of tearing of the surface. These traces take the form of a few hairs and the use of a magnifying glass is an advantage. A second possibility is a thin line of gum along the edge of the flap or small splashes of gum on the envelope. The gummed part of the flap may have a very flat appearance.

iii. The lower flap. In most cases the lower flap of the

envelope has a narrow edge free from gum (about 1/16 inch).
When steam is used there is tendency for this free edge to
curl and the gummed part of the flap has a concave appearance.

iv. Inside the envelope. Open the envelope completely by cutting
the top and side and examine the inside for traces of gum or
signs of tearing. Finally steam off the sealing flap and see if
there is any sign of the surface under the gum being torn.

4. Defensive Measures.

It is impossible to employ obvious methods which will confirm
suspicion; the best defence is to make opening as difficult as
possible.

a. Use poor-quality envelopes. Add gum to the flap to ensure
that it is firmly sealed. (Cheap Manila envelopes are most
suitable.)

b. Always use the same type of envelope.

c. Practise opening yourself until you become thoroughly
familiar with the likely traces.

d. Arrange some subtle danger-signal.

5. Seals.

The use of a seal on the envelope makes the job of opening more
difficult but in no way guarantees that it cannot be done by
an expert. As special materials are necessary it is impossible
for the agent to deal with them, but using a seal he may obtain
additional signs that his own correspondence is being examined.

a. The wax may be dull and rather darker in colour.

b. The paper round the wax may show signs of displaced wax.

c. There may be a faint trace of grease on the paper round
the seal.

d.   There may be small spots of white or other coloured powder on the seal itself.

In those cases where it is possible for the materials to be carried the method is as follows:

i.   Make a mould of the seal with the special cement. A thin cover of grease should be put on the seal before the liquid cement is used. This prevents the hardened mould from sticking to the seal.

ii.   Break the seal along the line of the flap and open the envelope in the usual way. Great care should be taken that as little steam as possible gets on the seal.

iii. Reseal the envelope and then heat the wax, taking care to smooth it out so that there is no evidence of the break. While the wax is still soft, use the mould to make the impression of the seal.

Note: Great care should be taken in the heating of the wax as it is very easy to scorch the paper round the seal and impossible to disguise the result.

DISPOSAL OF PARACHUTE.

INTRODUCTION.

The first thought of an agent on landing is the disposal of his parachute.

This disposal must be permanent, for discovery, whether it be immediate or many months later, will lead to:-

1.   Interrogation of all inhabitants (if any) in the vicinity and consequent tracing of collaborator and eventual arrest of the agent himself.

2. Enforced abandonment of the D.P.

BURIAL.

If there is a river or deep lake near-by, the problem of
disposal is immediately solved. Otherwise the safest method is
by burying.

If the following principles are followed there is little
likelihood of the parachute ever being found:-

1. Avoid ground under cultivation.

2. Digging should be done under cover. The spot for burial
should be chosen in a wood and as remote as possible from big
trees because roots are a serious handicap to quick and silent
digging.

3. The parachute should be temporarily hidden while the hole
is being dug.

4. Digging procedure. Before proceeding to dig, roll up
trousers to knee.

a). The dimensions of the hole must be approximately 2' long
by 2' wide 2' 6" deep, and this length and breadth should be
lightly marked out with a spade point.

b). Remove all loose material, such as leaves, twigs, pine
cones, etc. and keep carefully apart. If there are bramble
or ground ivy branches over the rectangle marked out, those
should be carefully pulled aside, but on no account broken
or damaged as they will be replaced and used as natural
camouflage later.

c). Cut down through the turf and top soil along all four sides
of the hole. This top should then be cut again either into

smaller rectangles or squares. The number of cuts made will depend on the nature of the top.

d). Remove each sod one by one and place, in exactly the same order as taken out, on a corner of the sheet or sacking provided, which should be spread out near the hole. This will ensure that the top sods are replaced in the correct order, which is so essential for even packing.

e). Digging should be done from the inside of the hole, that is, the digger must work standing in the hole itself. This will eliminate tell-tale trampling down of leaves etc. on the edges. All earth should be carefully put on to the sacking.

f). Having put the parachute into the hole, shovel in the earth in small quantities, stamping down quietly but firmly with both feet. The tighter the earth is packed the better, and before replacing the top turf make sure that there is absolutely no "give". The tighter the 'chute is rolled, the better. If there is any balloon effect, puncture with spade or knife.

g). Replace the top turf in correct order, packing it together with pressure of the fingers.

h). "Sprinkle" with loose leaves, twigs, etc. that were put carefully aside in the first place. This sprinkling should be done from a height of 5' to 6' as this will produce a more natural fall.

i). Dispose of surplus earth and the sacking at some distance away - water, rabbit holes are excellent places. Finally, brush and switch lightly with a leafy branch the area of the burying site for a distance of several yards all round. Trodden grass should be revived as possible by hand before switching.

CONCLUSION.

Finally, see that shoes are clean - although you may have been given a second pair.

SUBVERSIVE ORGANISATION EXERCISE.
(Minimum of 8 students).

Duration: 1-2 weeks.

Time: Commence at end of 1st week's instruction.

1 period to start the scheme and 1 for discussion at end.

OBJECT.

To give practice in:

1. Security methods - involving personal security and that of an organisation.

2. Detective methods:

a. Exposure of organisation by agents provocateurs.

b. Discovery of agents provocateurs by organisation.

GENERAL IDEA.

During this course you will regard yourselves - when not doing regular exercises, attending lectures, etc. - as being citizen in an enemy-occupied country.

Among you there is a group of agents provocateurs and also a group of subversive saboteurs. The remainder are members of the public.

The identity of the member of each group is entirely unknown to everybody. You will establish contact with one another according to the instructions which you will be given. This should be done as unobtrusively as possible, so that nobody knows who is in contact with whom, except those directly involved.

As the course progresses, advice, instructions, material etc. will be infiltrated to the groups by the D.O.

The highest degree of security will be maintained by both secret groups. The members of the public have no reason for being discreet because they are not necessarily sympathetic to either side. Neither group should be regarded either as Allied or German.

N.B.

1. The greatest discretion is required in the use of passwords, which must be introduced naturally into conversations because you may be talking to the wrong person.

2. Each side will seek to penetrate the other, impede its activities and discover its plans.

3. No arrests nor denunciations will be made; identities and suspicious activities should be reported to the respective lenders.

4. Leaders of both groups and members of the public will submit reports on their activities which will be discussed at the end of the scheme.

X. 7

TREASURE HUNT.

Duration: 2 hrs.

Object.

To give practice in:-

1. Deciphering of messages.

2. Construction of alibis.

3. Body searches.

4. Use of passwords.

5. Recognition of persons from given descriptions.

6. Knowledge of Enemy Forces.

This exercise is run in a series of stages and requires a minimum directional staff of four.

Fines of ten minutes or so are instituted for mistakes, failure to decode, etc.

Stage 1.

Students are given a message in code, which, when deciphered, gives clues to the second stage - the whereabouts of a map.

Stage 2.

Attached to the map are written instructions indicating a certain spot actually marked on the map, where a contact is waiting.

The identity of this contact will be established through a password.

Stage 3.

Students are asked by the contact to complete a test on knowledge of enemy forces; for instance, they may be given

147

a series of photographs to recognise or they may be asked
to draw an organisation plan of the Nazi Party or German
Police.

This contact will give verbal directions to proceed to some
other spot where there is yet another contact, and will also
give them a message to memorise.

(A variation may be introduced before this contact by having
an instructor who is unknown to the students and dressed
in civilian clothes, near the R.V. He will give a similar,
but wrong, answer to the password. This tests the students'
reactions to an unforeseen situation.)

Stage 4.

The students repeat the message to the contact, and, in
addition, have to assemble various stripped weapons. When
this has been completed, the contact will give directions
to proceed to a spot where dummy explosives are hidden. Each
student must conceal explosives about his person and must
return to his house via a certain entrance, which represents a
police control post.

Stage 5.

At the entrance indicated, students go through a frisk search,
and they are given a brief interrogation on where they have
been. The students are then told to report to a certain room
in their house.

Stage 6.

Students are asked to describe one of their contacts.

After the addition of fines, placing results are put on the
blackboard.

RECONNAISSANCE AND SELECTION OF DROPPING POINTS FOR PARACHUTE OPERATIONS.

Reference Map:

> Duration: 2-3 hrs.
>
> Time:

OBJECT.

To give students practice in choosing suitable dropping points
for parachute operations from the map and verifying their
choice by reconnaissance on the ground.

LESSONS TO BE LEARNT.

However detailed a map, personal reconnaissance is essential
if safe and secure ground is to be selected.

Avoidance of:

a. Trees which would obscure the lights.

b. Overhead wires.

c. Rough and broken ground for landing personnel.

d. Reliance on woods, which may have been cut down, as
landmarks.

Students are given a map of the local area, and are given a
limited space within which they may select suitable dropping
points in accordance with principles already given to them in
Lecture B.3.

Students are then taken out in transport and they make a
detailed reconnaissance of the areas they have chosen by
walking across country.

Students should be asked to judge the strength of the wind
from the highest point in the neighbourhood and to state what
drift they would allow and in what direction.

FIELDCRAFT.

1. How to find your way in woods and close country.

a). Examine moss on trees; tilt of the trees; trees uprooted by
storm (Note: In England moss is generally on west side; trees
generally tilt to the east).

b). Examine tracks of domestic animals. These usually lead to
a village or to water. In early morning, if pads on tracks are
fresh, they lead away from a village; at dusk the reverse.

c). Remember, village dogs can give away your presence;
approach them upwind.

d). To ensure finding the same way back, break a few twigs on
trees, so that they hang down every hundred yards or so; make
an occasional arrow-head with stones; leave sticks pointing in
the right direction.

2.   Where to hide.

a).   By day.

i).   Hollow tree, or tree with a good platform or suitable
bough.

ii). Evergreen bush.

iii). Hay or straw stacks (good O.P.s).

iv). Pit holes in fields.

v).   May to September in hay or cornfields (always enter the
way it is drilled).

b).   By night. Safest in the open.

i).   Hay and straw stacks.

ii). Evergreen boughs.

iii). Bracken or heather.

3.   How to detect presence of other persons.

a).   By day.

i).   Tie dark cotton thread across track, one foot from ground.

ii). Level ground (e.g. mole hill) with a branch.

iii). When wind towards you, drop a few dead sticks in your
track.

iv). Watch both domestic or wild animals. If a stranger
approaches they will all look the same way. (Cows start
mooing, sheep bleating, etc.)

b).   By night. If a stranger approaches:

i).   Rabbits will make a thumping sound on the ground, deer will give a kind of bark.

ii). Pigeons are very easily disturbed and easily leave their roosts.

iii). Plovers call out.

iv). If you lie flat and put your ear to the ground, you will hear footsteps, and be able to see quite a distance on the darkest night.

4.   Where to live in the open.

a).   Edge of woods.

b).   Disused quarries.

c).   Chalk or gravel pits.

d).   An old lime kiln.

How to make a shelter.

Materials: boughs of evergreen or pine about four feet long; eight poles about six feet long and one inch in diameter.

Method of construction: Lay two poles on the ground about two feet apart, cover with boughs, then lay two more poles on the top. Tie these at both ends and in the middle. Make another set as before. Erect the two sides length-ways to form an inverted "V". Line the bottom with boughs to form a mattress; covering can be made with rushes, straw, bracken or heather. In the day time, the shelter should be laid flat on the ground out of sight.

5.   Food and water.

a).   How to find water.

i.   In valleys on south side of hills.

ii. Near rushes, willow trees, etc.

iii. Presence of cattle and sheep.

iv. In eastern countries, natives sing at night when working oxen on irrigation waterwheel.

b). Finding food.

i. Catching birds by snares, traps, gins, fishhooks, etc.

ii. Catching rabbits by snares, traps, gins, nets etc.

iii. Where to find deer and how to stalk them (demonstrations for (i) and (ii)).

c). Finding eggs.

i. Waterhens' eggs. By side of dykes, ponds and in rushes.

ii. Pheasants' eggs. In woods and hedgerows, April to May. How to tell when good to eat. The bigger the clutch the more likely they are to be good.

iii. English or grey partridges. In hedgerows, but difficult to find as they are covered.

iv. French or Red Leg partridges. As for (ii).

v. Plovers' eggs. On rough land or pasture. How to tell when good to eat.

6. How to make a fire.
a). The best fire for boiling, frying or grilling on a spit is the Gypsy fire which is made by standing up short thin pieces of wood in the shape of a bell tent. Ash, oak, birch, fir, gorse, beech, elm and thorn all kindle well, but thorn gives off a strong scent which can be detected some distance away. In country where wood is unavailable, dried cattle or horse dung can be used.

To hang a kettle or billy-tin over the fire, two crotch sticks
and cross stick are necessary. Always light fire, if possible,
before daylight to avoid smoke being seen; cooking can then be
done by the cinders.

b). Ovens.

A small trench about three feet long is useful. A good oven
can be made from a four or five gallon tin, provided it is
water-tight. Clean out well and lay it on its side on bricks
or large stones high enough to allow of a fire underneath.
Leave the open end facing west; make a chimney about two feet
high at the other. Cover oven with about a foot of clay or mud
mixed with water to a stiff paste. Allow this to dry in the
air for one day, and light only a small fire under it on the
next. This will finally dry it off. With an enamel plate or
mess tin, anything can be baked in this oven.

7. Cooking.

a). How to make bread. Mix $\frac{1}{2}$ lb. or more of flour with water or
milk to a stiff dough; add a pinch of salt and a spoonful of
baking powder if available. Put in oven (see 6. (b)) and cook
for one hour.

b). Partridges will take $\frac{3}{4}$ hour to cook in the oven; pheasants
and ducks $1\frac{1}{2}$ hours.

c). Hares and rabbits are best stewed. Always clean out rabbits
and deer as soon as possible after killing.

d). Chuppaties: mix $\frac{1}{2}$ lb. or more of flour with water to a
stiff paste, add a pinch of salt then roll out like a pancake.
They should be cooked on an ember fire on a steel or enamel
plate. Keep turning as for pancakes; they will take ten
minutes to cook and are improved by a layer of jam.